GRAPHIC LIBRARY™

GRAPHIC SCIENCE

DECODING GENES

WITH

MAX AXIOM™
SUPER SCIENTIST

4D An Augmented Reading Science Experience

by Amber J. Keyser, PhD | illustrated by Tod G. Smith and Al Milgrom

Consultant:
Monte Westerfield, PhD
Professor of Biology
University of Oregon

CAPSTONE PRESS
a capstone imprint

Graphic Library is published by Capstone Press,
1710 Roe Crest Drive, North Mankato, Minnesota 56003.
www.capstonepub.com

Library of Congress Cataloging-in-Publication Data is available on the Library of Congress website.

ISBN: 978-1-5435-7247-6 (library binding)
ISBN: 978-1-5435-7545-3 (paperback)
ISBN: 978-1-5435-7251-3 (eBook PDF)

Summary: In graphic novel format, follows the adventures of Max Axiom
as he explains the science behind genes.

Designer
Alison Thiele

Colorist
Matt Webb

Production Specialist
Laura Manthe

Cover Colorist
Krista Ward

Media Researcher
Wanda Winch

Editor
Mari Bolte

Photo Credits
Capstone Studio: Karon Dubke, 29, back cover

All internet sites appearing in back matter were available and accurate
when this book was sent to press.

1 Ask an adult to download the app.

Capstone 4D
Education

2 Scan any page with the star.

3 Enjoy your cool stuff!

————— OR —————

Use this password at capstone4D.com

genes.72476

Printed in the United States of America.
PA70

TABLE OF CONTENTS

SECTION 1

SECTION 2

SECTION 3

SECTION 4

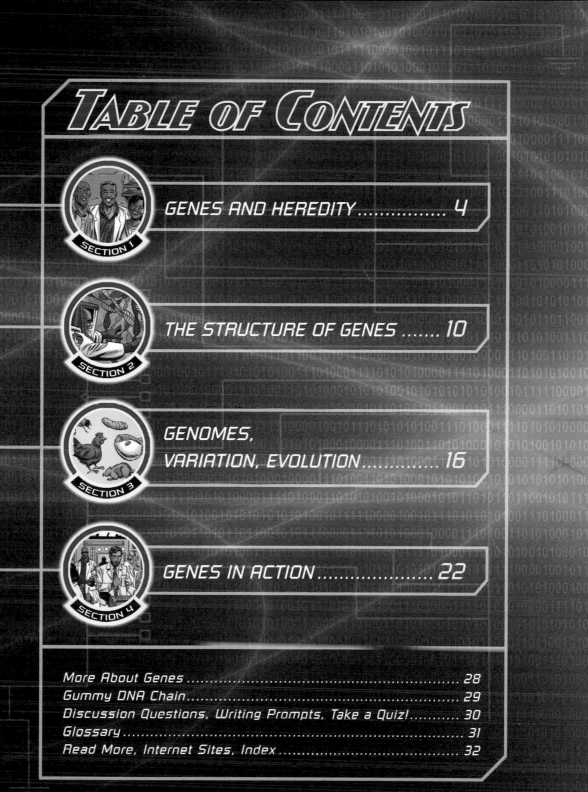

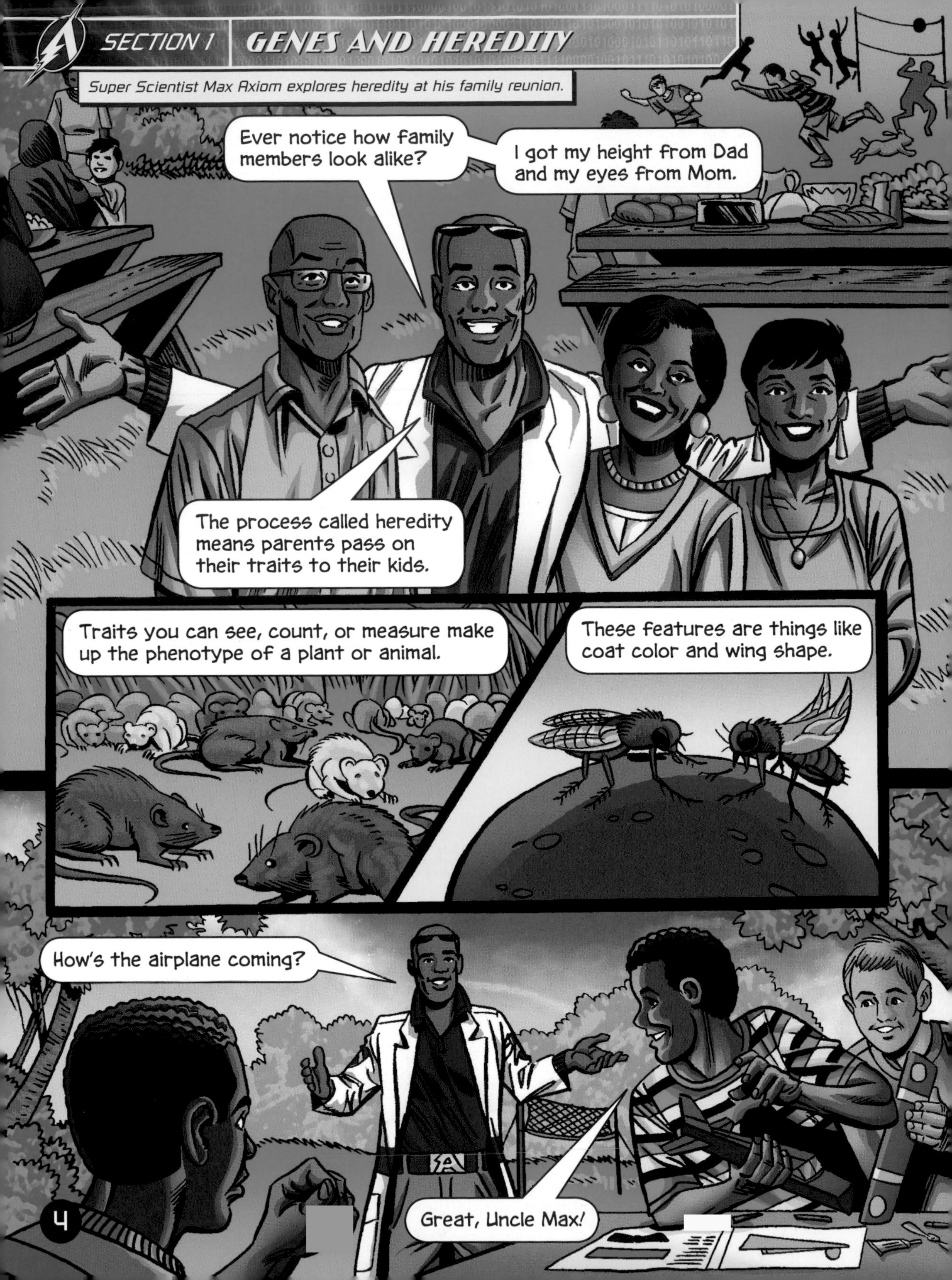
SECTION 1 GENES AND HEREDITY
Super Scientist Max Axiom explores heredity at his family reunion.
Ever notice how family members look alike?
I got my height from Dad and my eyes from Mom.
The process called heredity means parents pass on their traits to their kids.
Traits you can see, count, or measure make up the phenotype of a plant or animal.
These features are things like coat color and wing shape.
How's the airplane coming?
Great, Uncle Max!

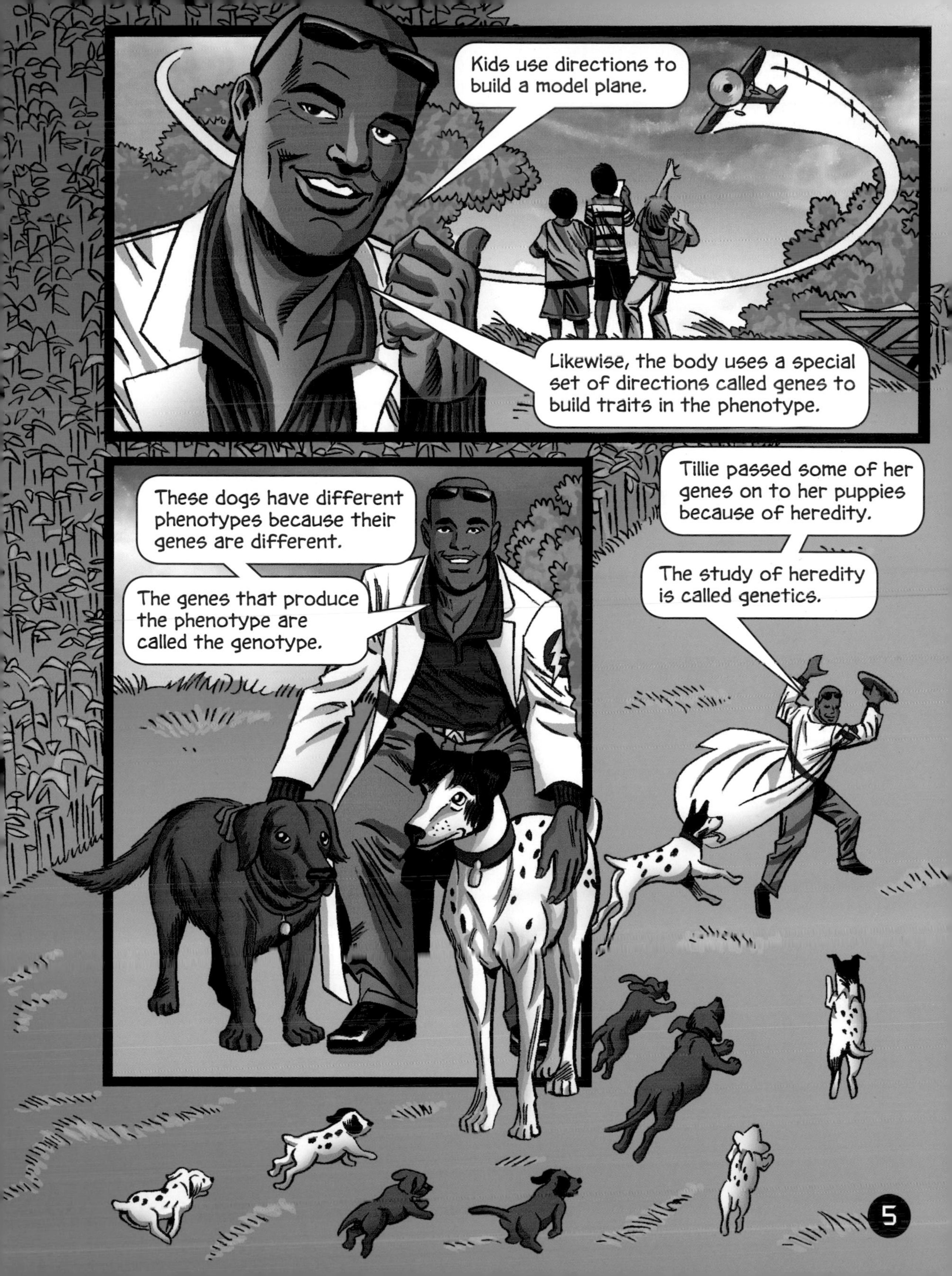

Kids use directions to build a model plane.
Likewise, the body uses a special set of directions called genes to build traits in the phenotype.
These dogs have different phenotypes because their genes are different.
The genes that produce the phenotype are called the genotype.
Tillie passed some of her genes on to her puppies because of heredity.
The study of heredity is called genetics.

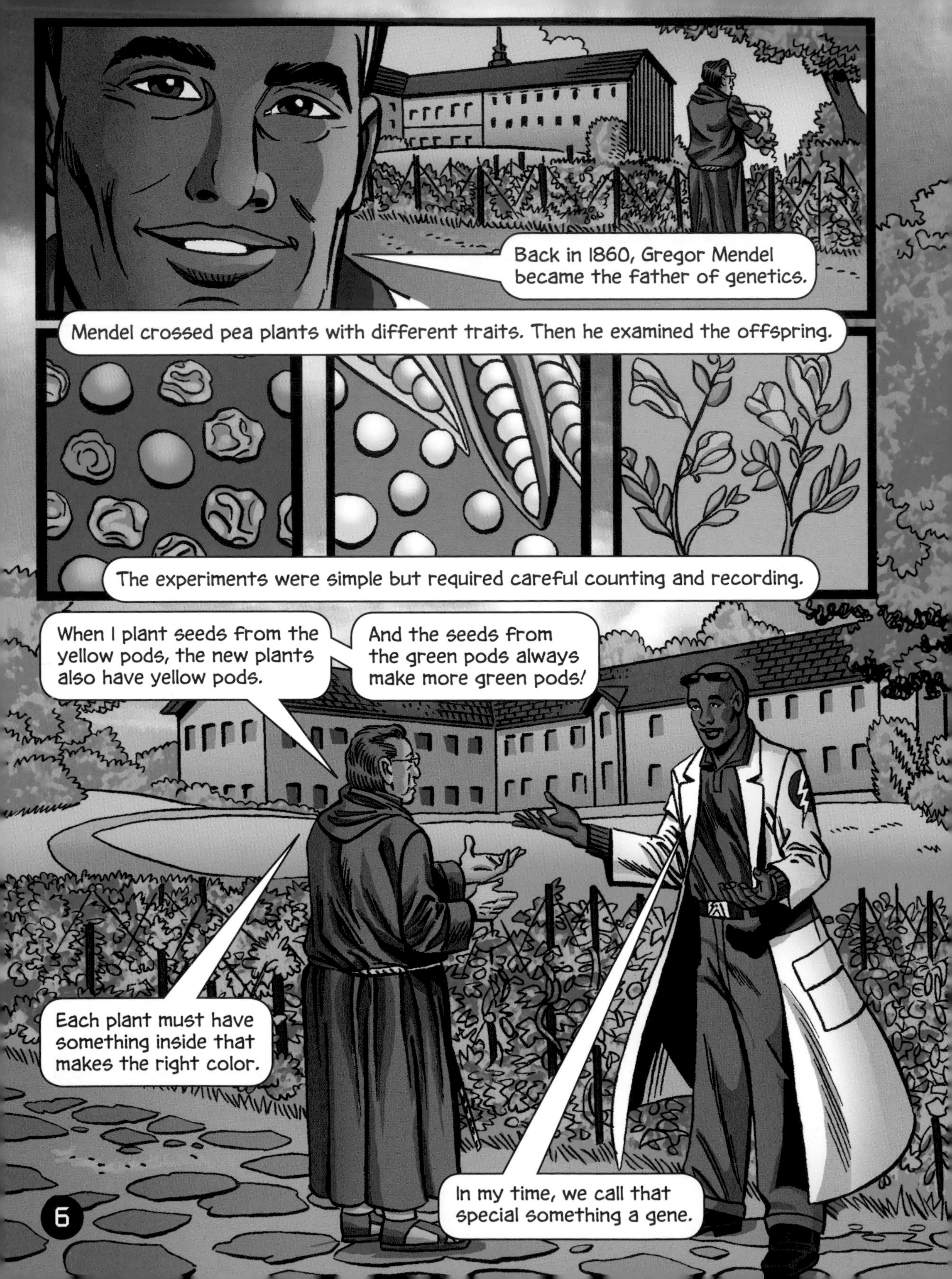

Back in 1860, Gregor Mendel became the father of genetics.
Mendel crossed pea plants with different traits. Then he examined the offspring.
The experiments were simple but required careful counting and recording.
When I plant seeds from the yellow pods, the new plants also have yellow pods.
And the seeds from the green pods always make more green pods!
Each plant must have something inside that makes the right color.
In my time, we call that special something a gene.

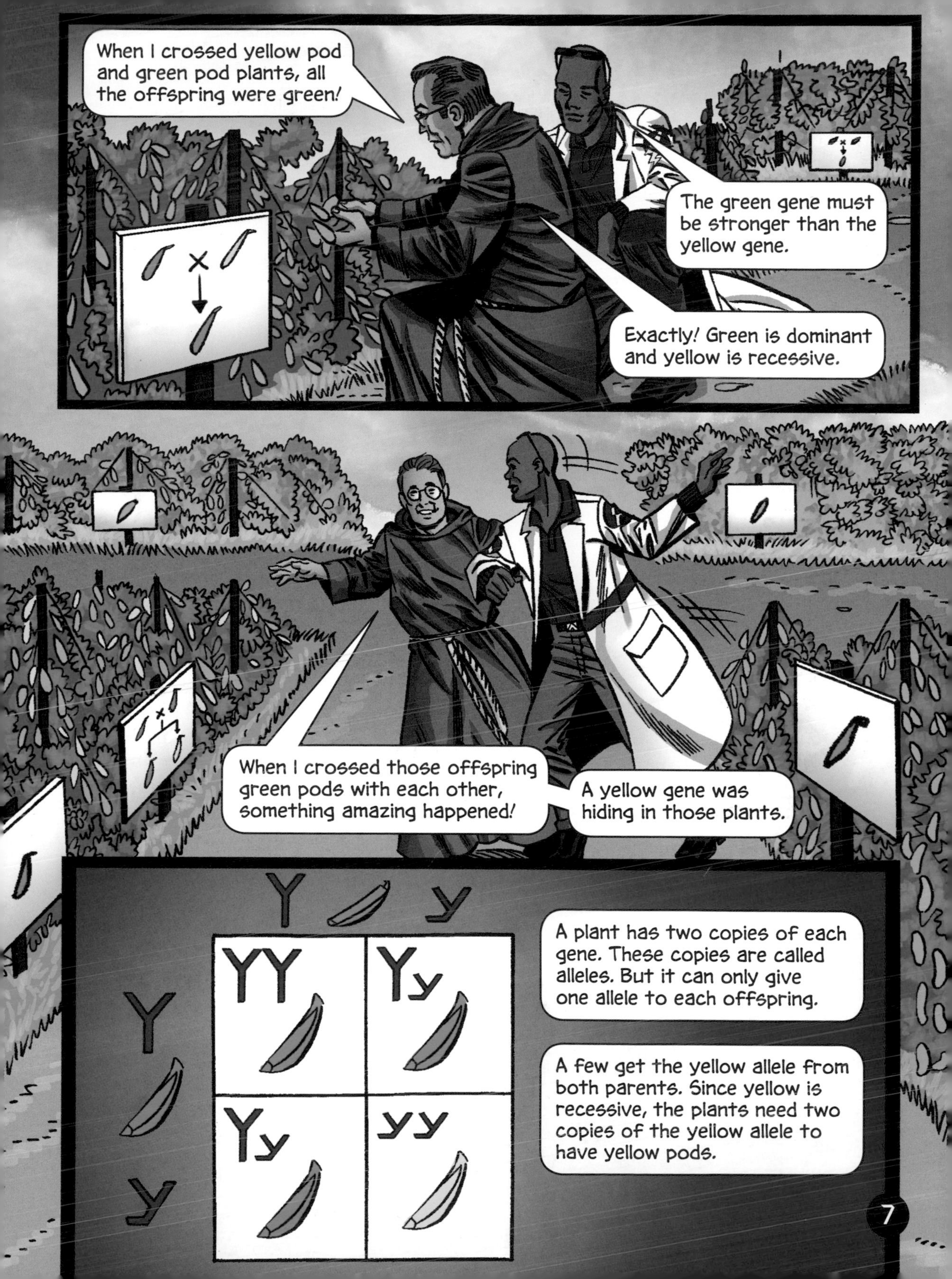
When I crossed yellow pod and green pod plants, all the offspring were green!
The green gene must be stronger than the yellow gene.
Exactly! Green is dominant and yellow is recessive.
When I crossed those offspring green pods with each other, something amazing happened!
A yellow gene was hiding in those plants.
Y
y
Y
y
YY
Yy
Yy
yy
A plant has two copies of each gene. These copies are called alleles. But it can only give one allele to each offspring.
A few get the yellow allele from both parents. Since yellow is recessive, the plants need two copies of the yellow allele to have yellow pods.

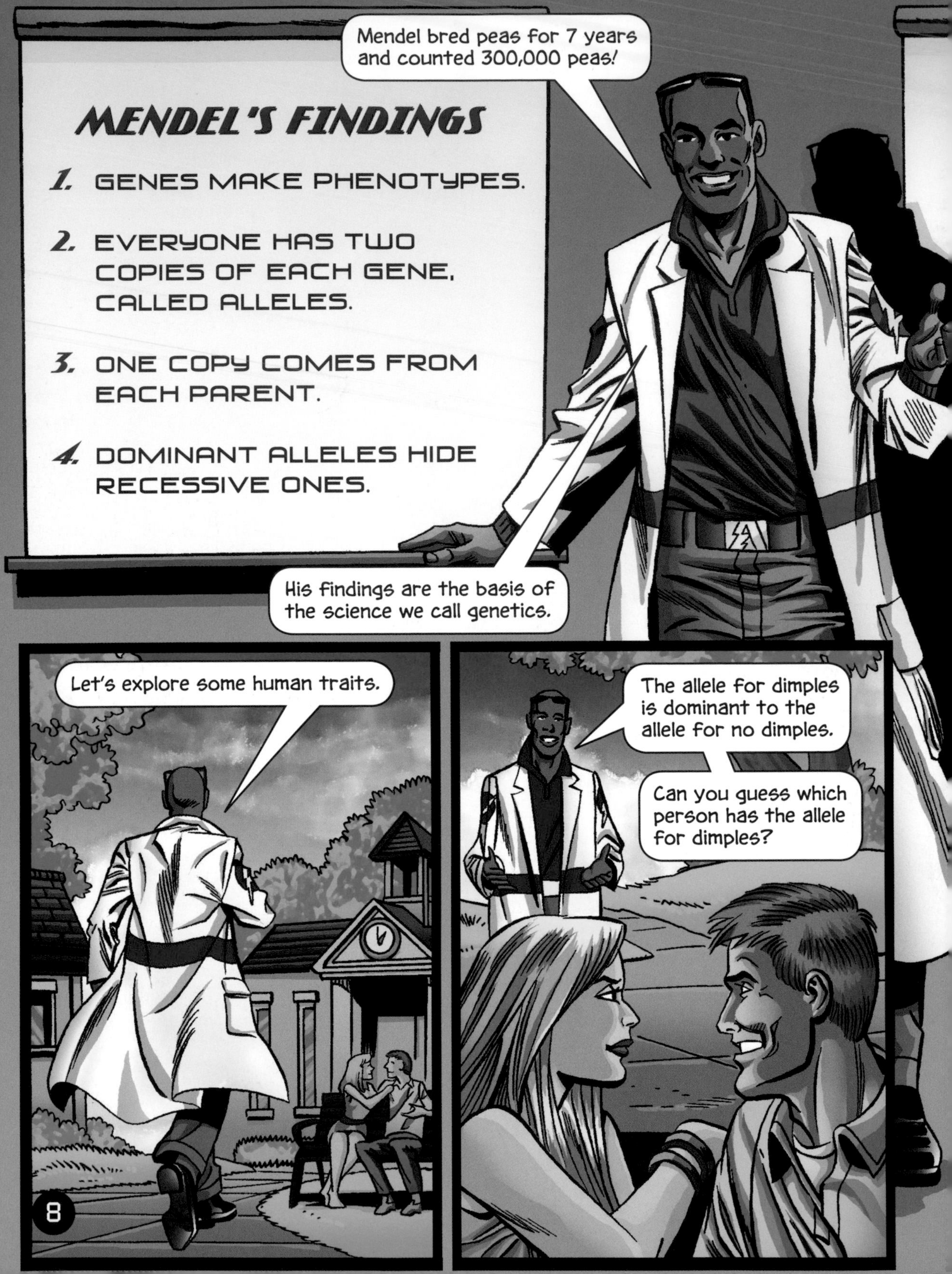

MENDEL'S FINDINGS
1. GENES MAKE PHENOTYPES.
2. EVERYONE HAS TWO COPIES OF EACH GENE, CALLED ALLELES.
3. ONE COPY COMES FROM EACH PARENT.
4. DOMINANT ALLELES HIDE RECESSIVE ONES.
Mendel bred peas for 7 years and counted 300,000 peas!
His findings are the basis of the science we call genetics.
Let's explore some human traits.
The allele for dimples is dominant to the allele for no dimples.
Can you guess which person has the allele for dimples?

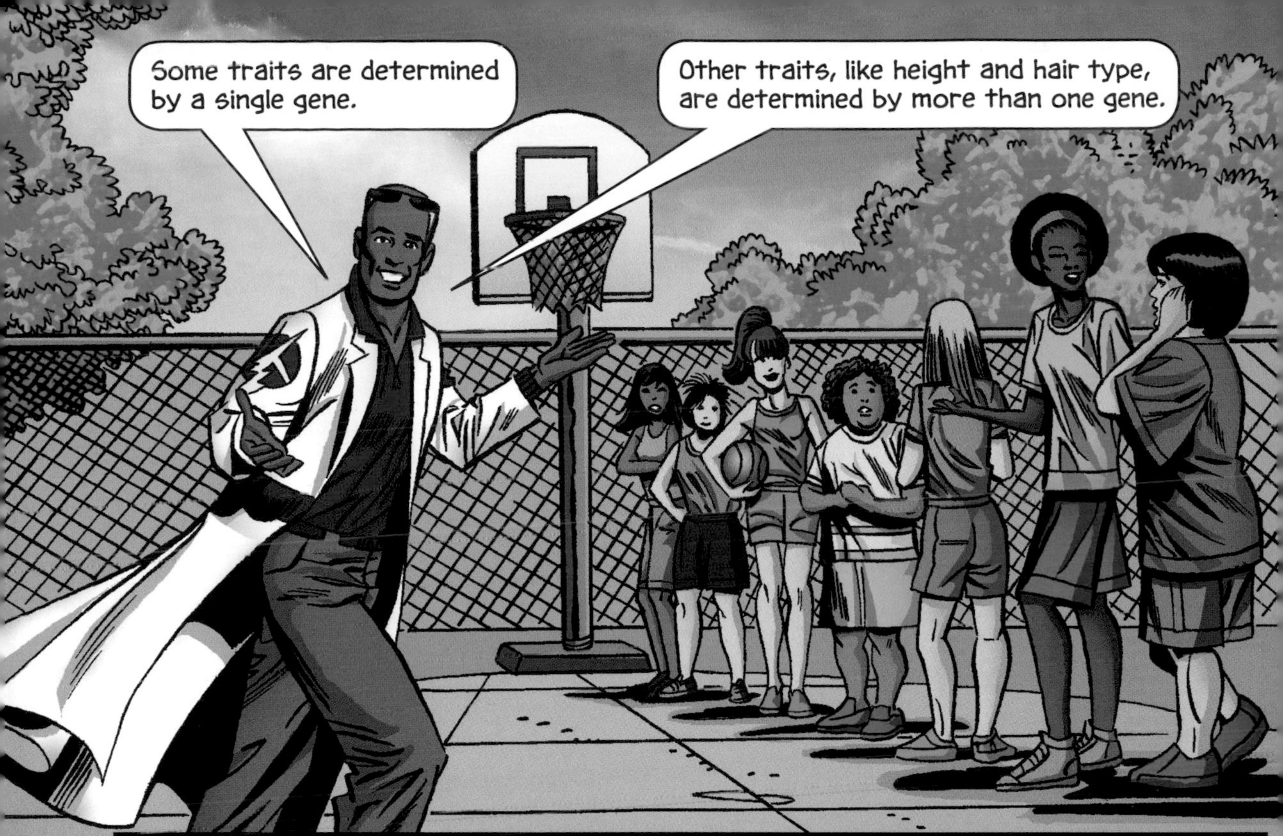
Some traits are determined by a single gene.
Other traits, like height and hair type, are determined by more than one gene.

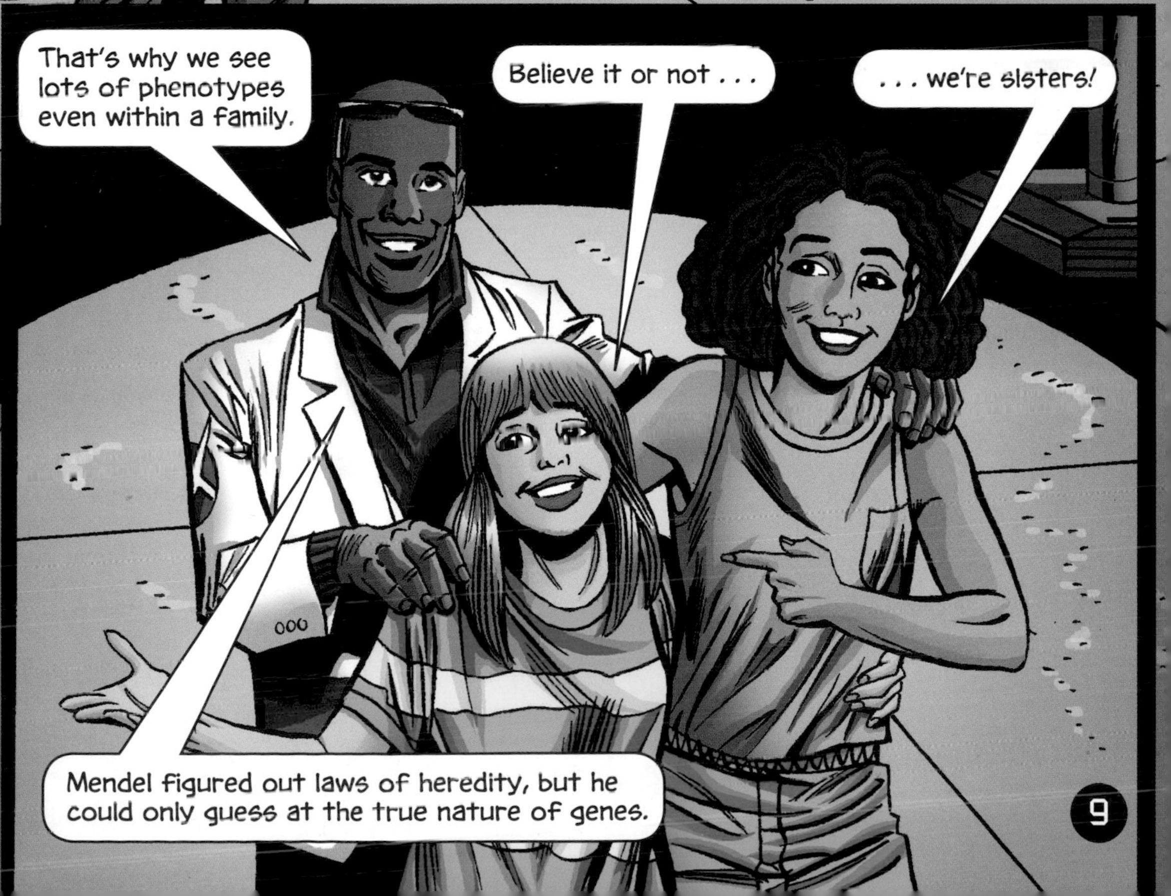
That's why we see lots of phenotypes even within a family.
Believe it or not . . .
. . . we're sisters!
Mendel figured out laws of heredity, but he could only guess at the true nature of genes.

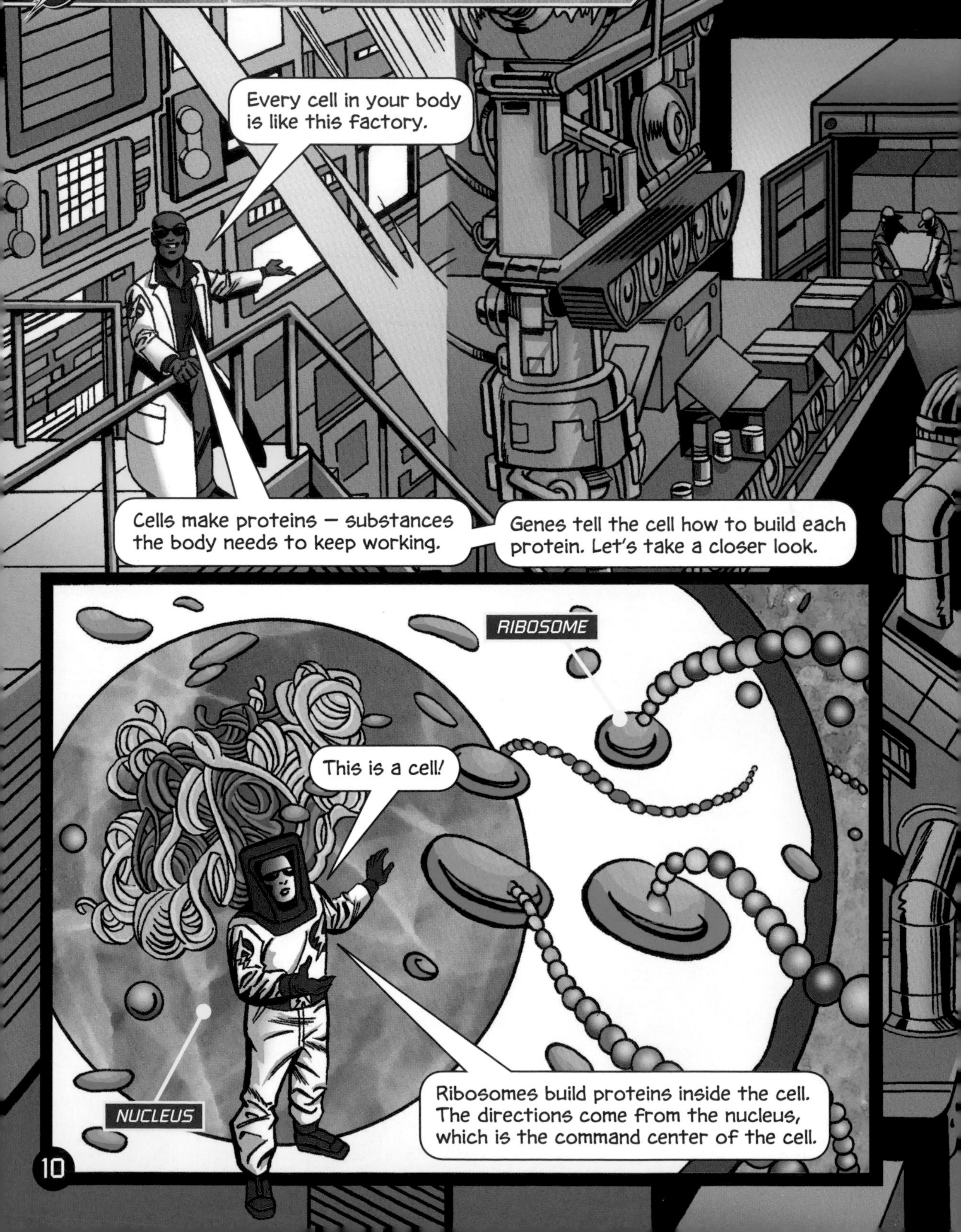
Every cell in your body is like this factory.
Cells make proteins — substances the body needs to keep working.
Genes tell the cell how to build each protein. Let's take a closer look.
RIBOSOME
This is a cell!
NUCLEUS
Ribosomes build proteins inside the cell. The directions come from the nucleus, which is the command center of the cell.

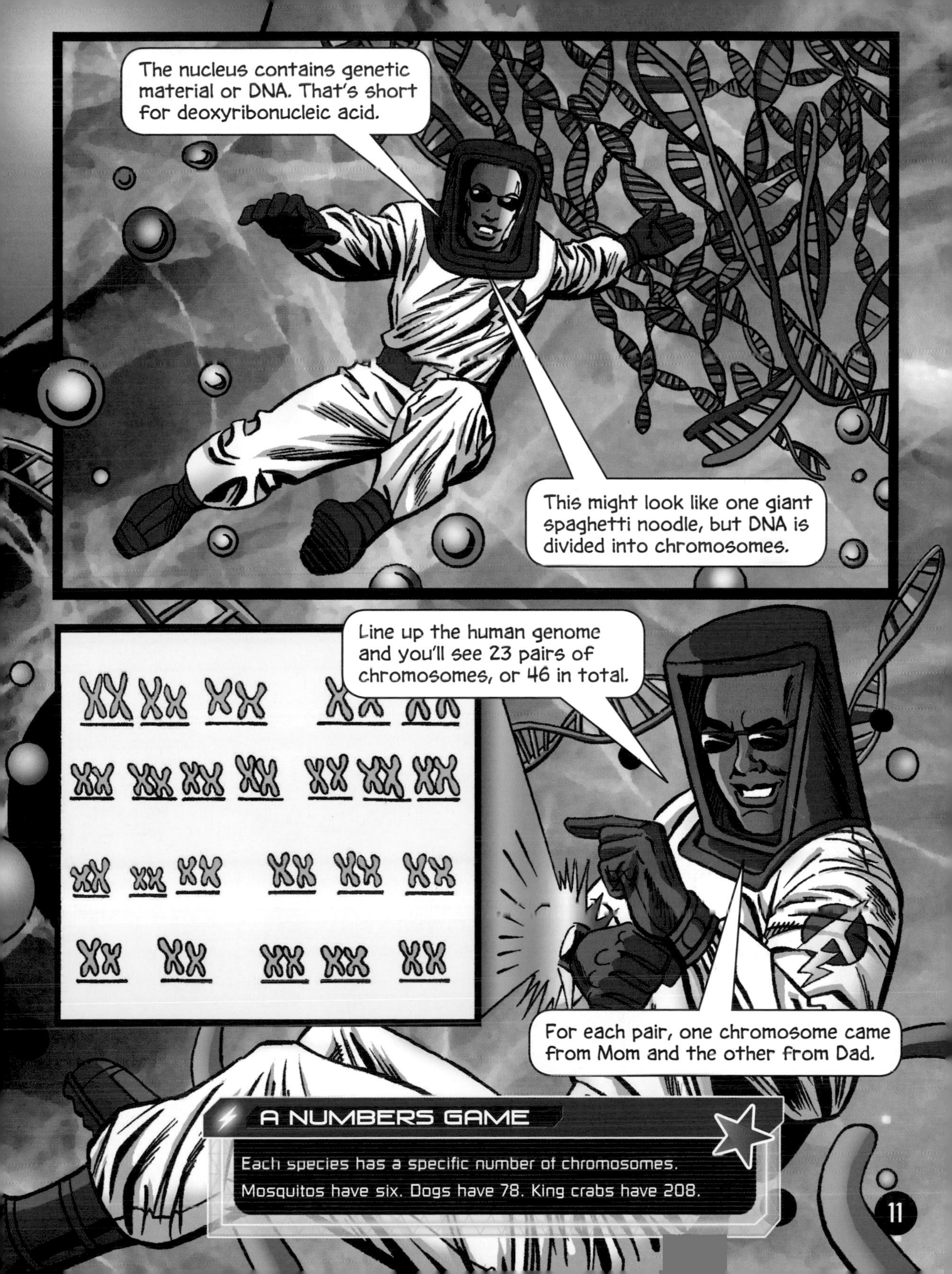

The nucleus contains genetic material or DNA. That's short for deoxyribonucleic acid.
This might look like one giant spaghetti noodle, but DNA is divided into chromosomes.
Line up the human genome and you'll see 23 pairs of chromosomes, or 46 in total.
For each pair, one chromosome came from Mom and the other from Dad.
A NUMBERS GAME
Each species has a specific number of chromosomes. Mosquitos have six. Dogs have 78. King crabs have 208.

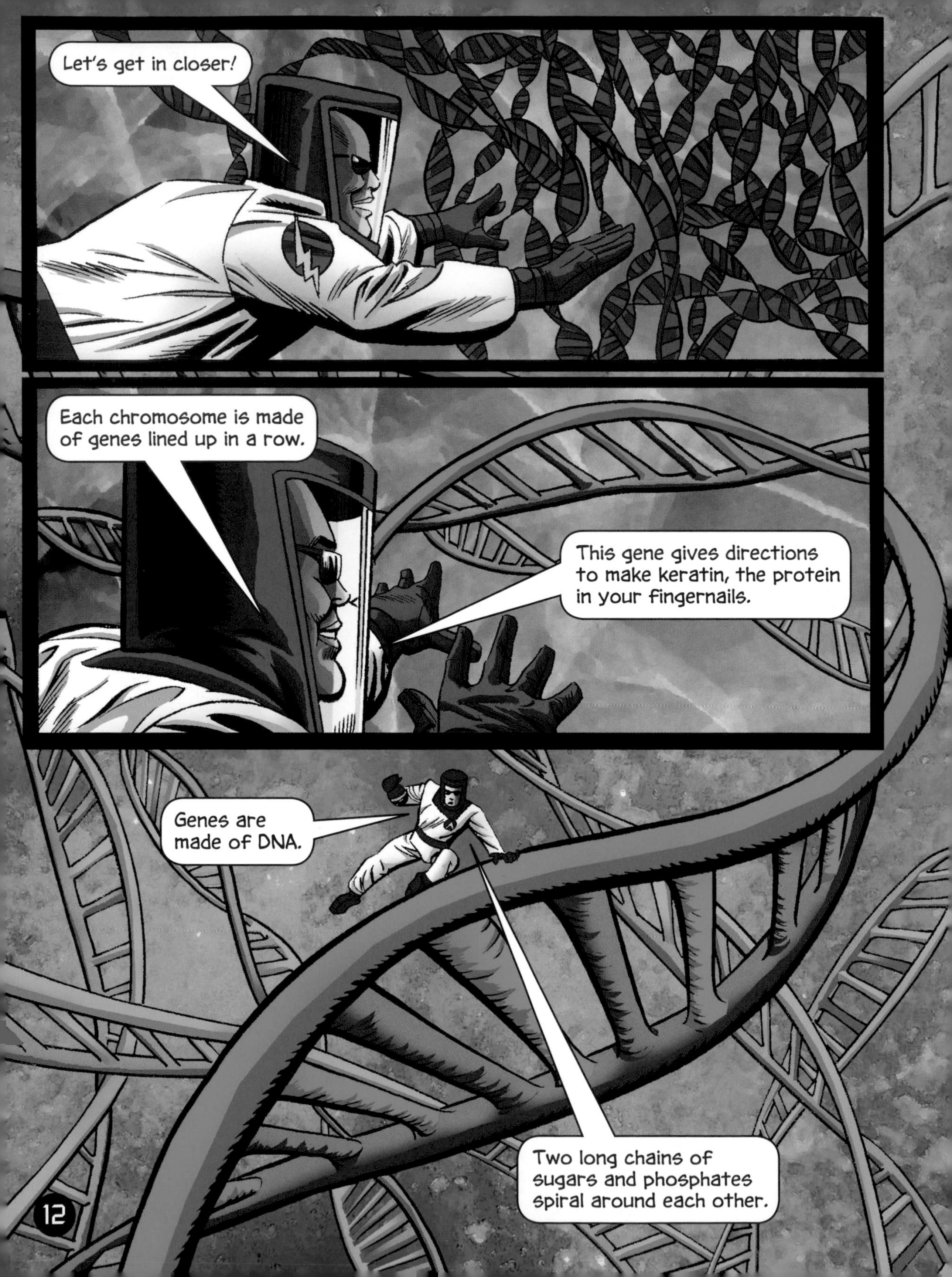
Let's get in closer!
Each chromosome is made of genes lined up in a row.
This gene gives directions to make keratin, the protein in your fingernails.
Genes are made of DNA.
Two long chains of sugars and phosphates spiral around each other.

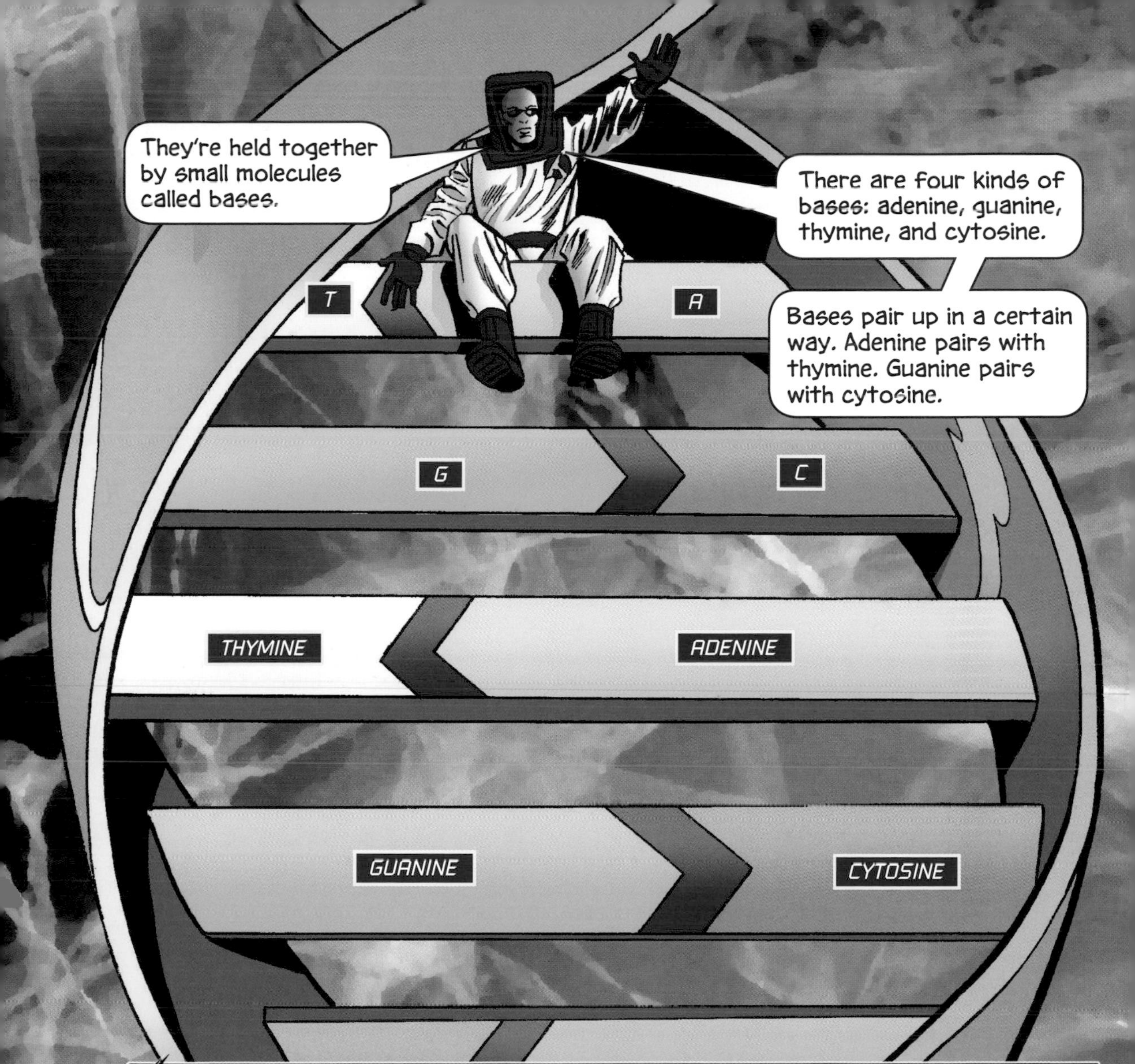
They're held together by small molecules called bases.
There are four kinds of bases: adenine, guanine, thymine, and cytosine.
Bases pair up in a certain way. Adenine pairs with thymine. Guanine pairs with cytosine.
T
A
G
C
THYMINE
ADENINE
GUANINE
CYTOSINE

STRUCTURE OF DNA

ACCESS GRANTED: MAX AXIOM

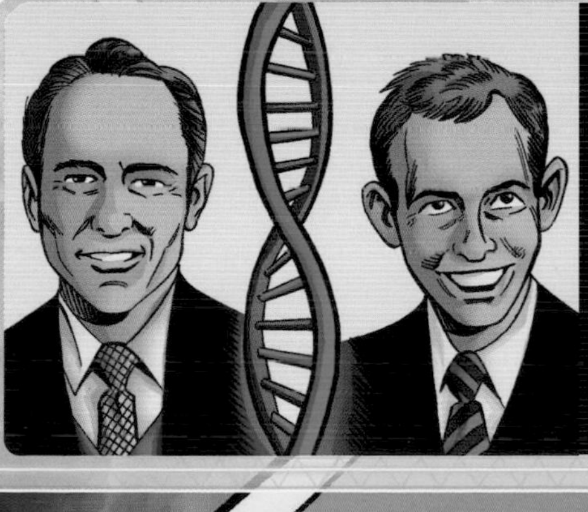

In 1953, Francis Crick and James Watson discovered the structure of DNA. By doing this, they won a great scientific race to unravel the puzzle of heredity. Both later acknowledged that they couldn't have done it without Rosalind Franklin's help. She took a special picture of DNA using X-ray crystallography.

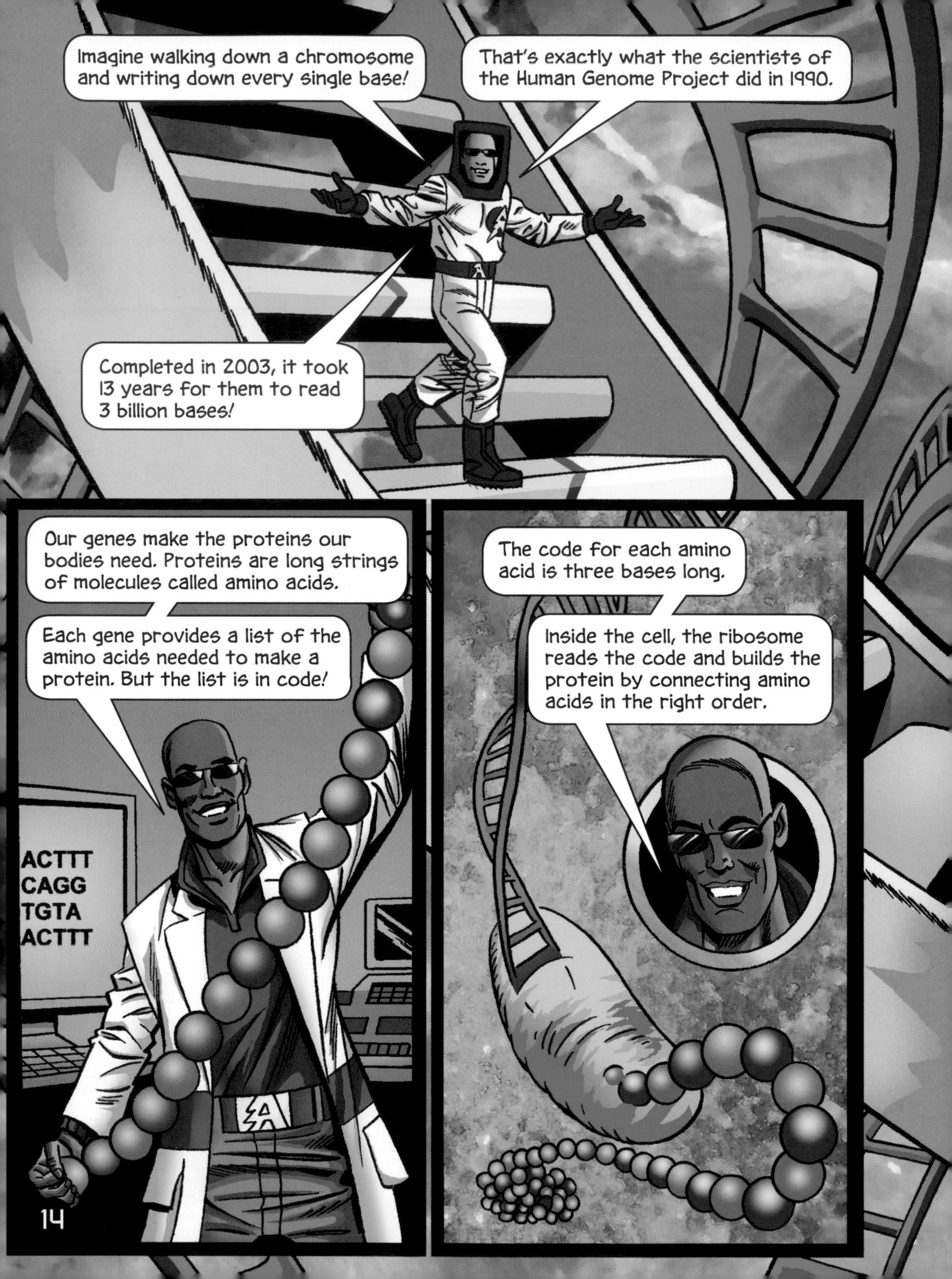
Imagine walking down a chromosome and writing down every single base!
That's exactly what the scientists of the Human Genome Project did in 1990.
Completed in 2003, it took 13 years for them to read 3 billion bases!
Our genes make the proteins our bodies need. Proteins are long strings of molecules called amino acids.
Each gene provides a list of the amino acids needed to make a protein. But the list is in code!
ACTTT
CAGG
TGTA
ACTTT
The code for each amino acid is three bases long.
Inside the cell, the ribosome reads the code and builds the protein by connecting amino acids in the right order.

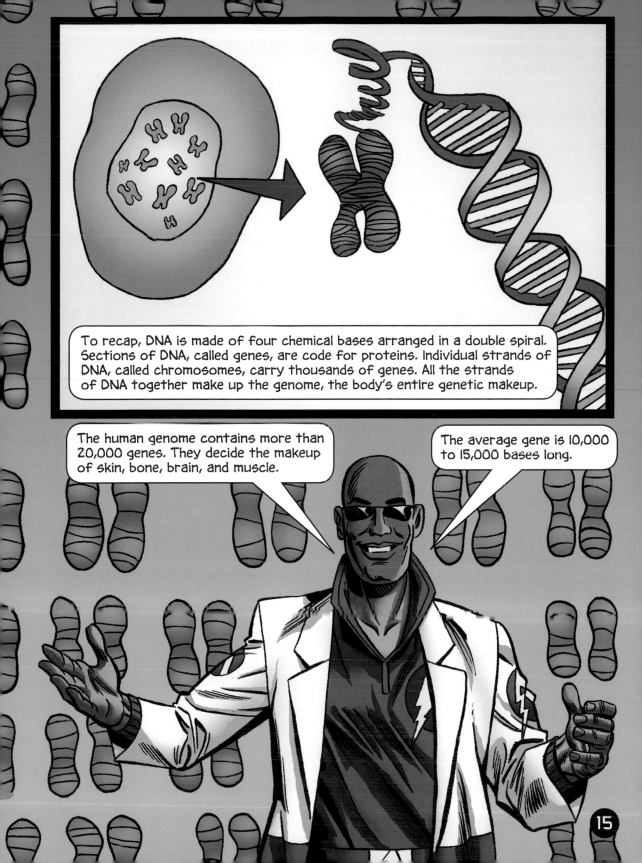

To recap, DNA is made of four chemical bases arranged in a double spiral. Sections of DNA, called genes, are code for proteins. Individual strands of DNA, called chromosomes, carry thousands of genes. All the strands of DNA together make up the genome, the body's entire genetic makeup.

The human genome contains more than 20,000 genes. They decide the makeup of skin, bone, brain, and muscle.

The average gene is 10,000 to 15,000 bases long.

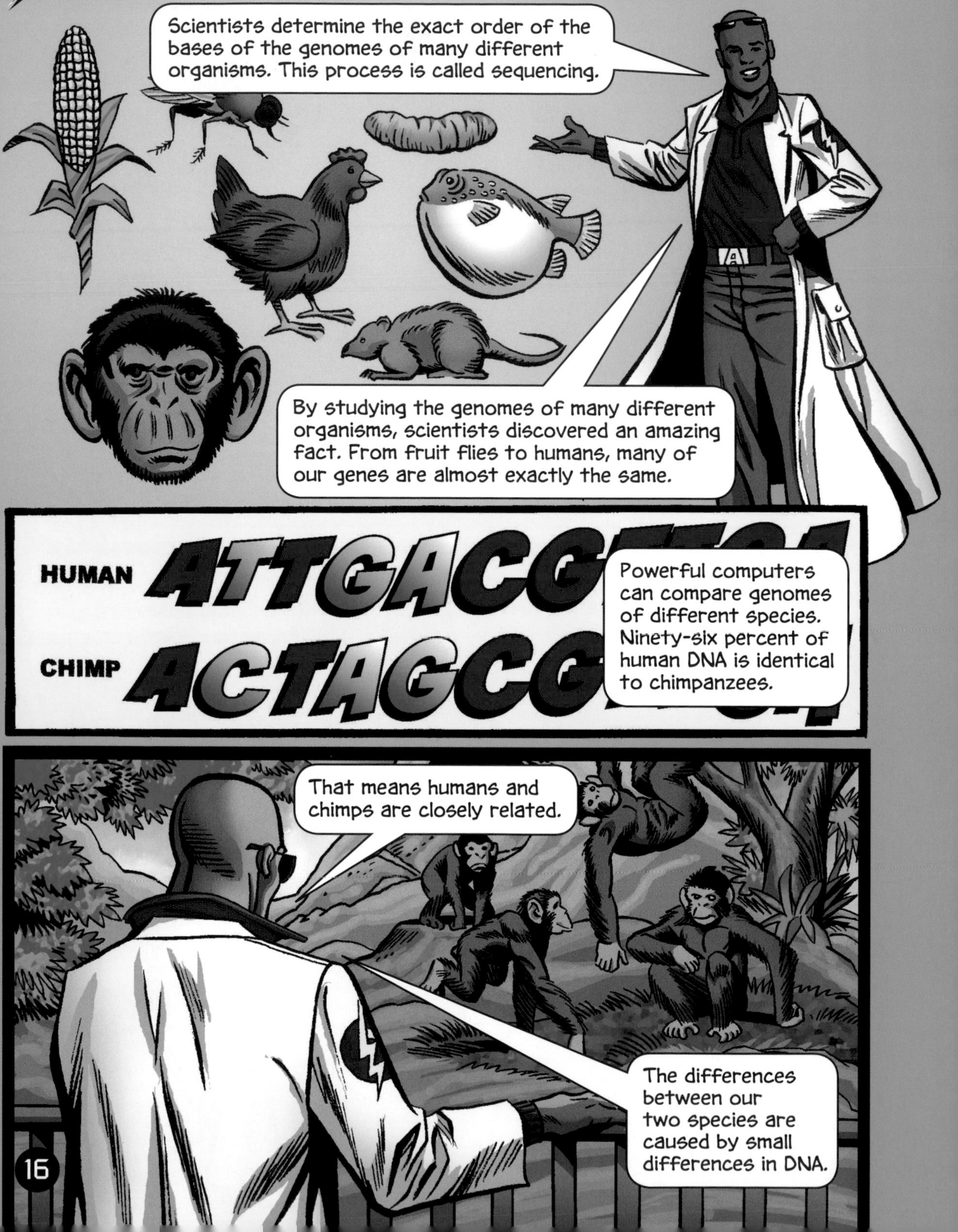
Scientists determine the exact order of the bases of the genomes of many different organisms. This process is called sequencing.
By studying the genomes of many different organisms, scientists discovered an amazing fact. From fruit flies to humans, many of our genes are almost exactly the same.
HUMAN
CHIMP
Powerful computers can compare genomes of different species. Ninety-six percent of human DNA is identical to chimpanzees.
That means humans and chimps are closely related.
The differences between our two species are caused by small differences in DNA.

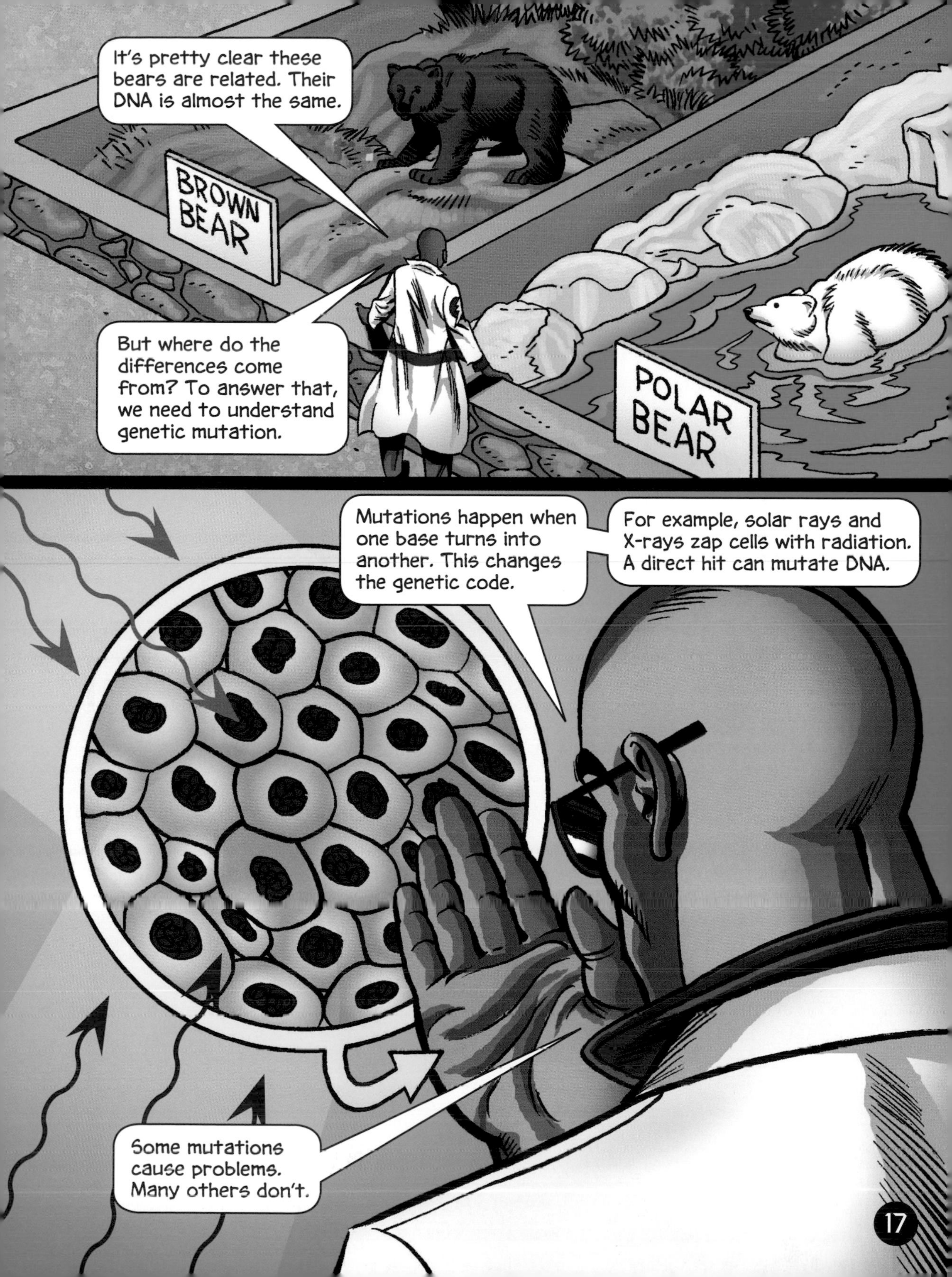

It's pretty clear these bears are related. Their DNA is almost the same.
BROWN BEAR
But where do the differences come from? To answer that, we need to understand genetic mutation.
POLAR BEAR
Mutations happen when one base turns into another. This changes the genetic code.
For example, solar rays and X-rays zap cells with radiation. A direct hit can mutate DNA.
Some mutations cause problems. Many others don't.

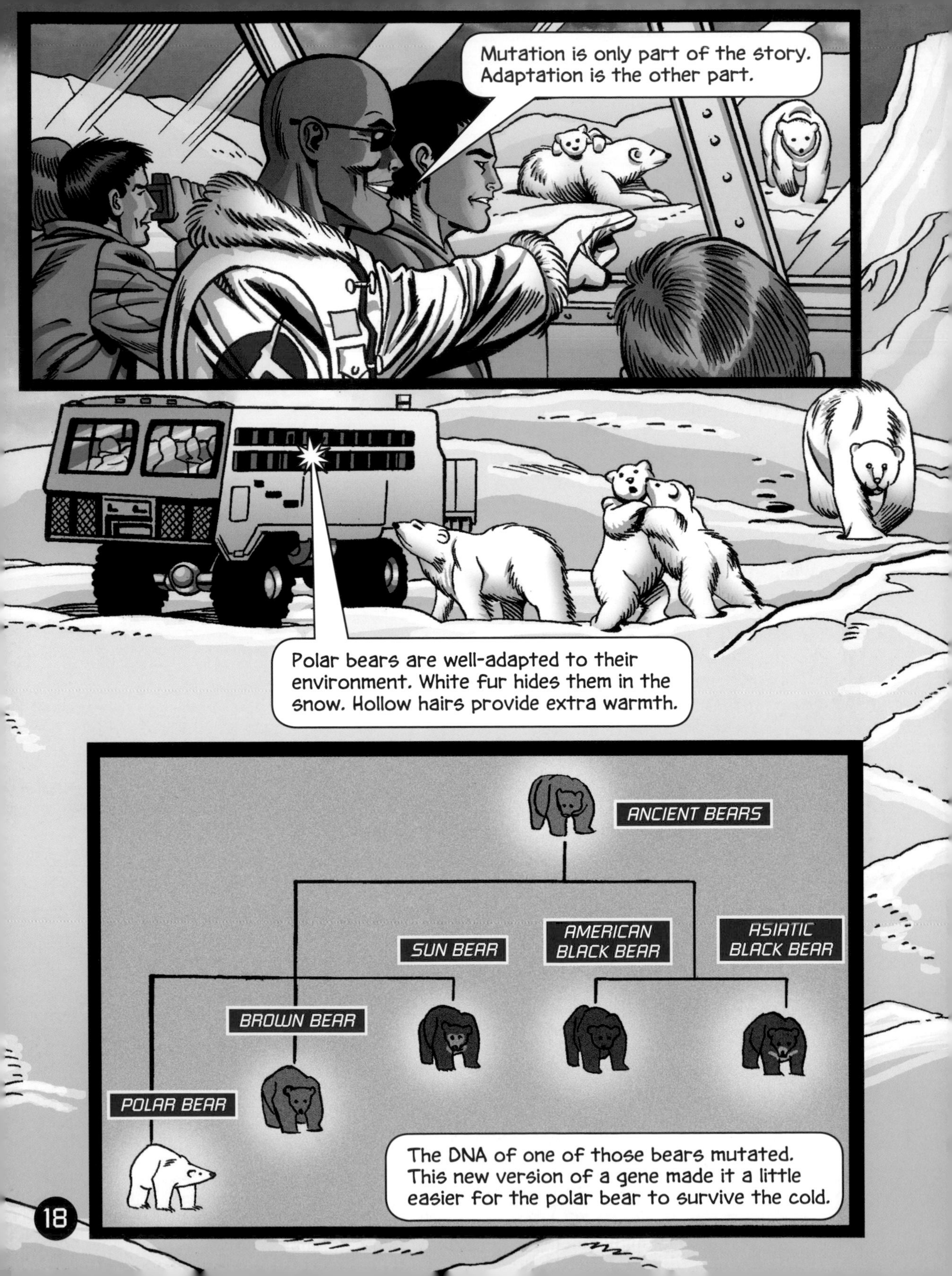

Mutation is only part of the story. Adaptation is the other part.
Polar bears are well-adapted to their environment. White fur hides them in the snow. Hollow hairs provide extra warmth.
ANCIENT BEARS
SUN BEAR
AMERICAN BLACK BEAR
ASIATIC BLACK BEAR
BROWN BEAR
POLAR BEAR
The DNA of one of those bears mutated. This new version of a gene made it a little easier for the polar bear to survive the cold.

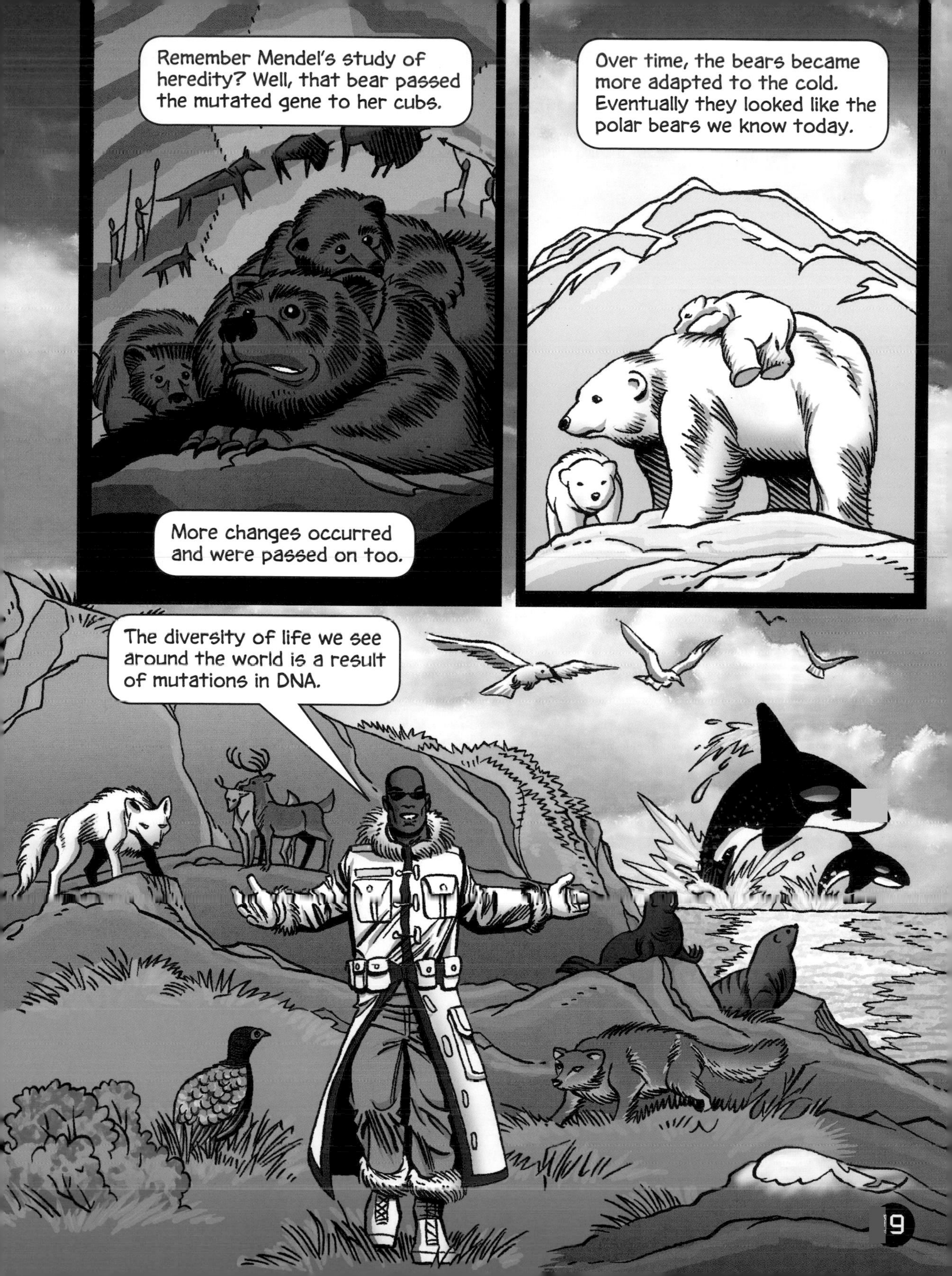
Remember Mendel's study of heredity? Well, that bear passed the mutated gene to her cubs.
More changes occurred and were passed on too.
Over time, the bears became more adapted to the cold. Eventually they looked like the polar bears we know today.
The diversity of life we see around the world is a result of mutations in DNA.

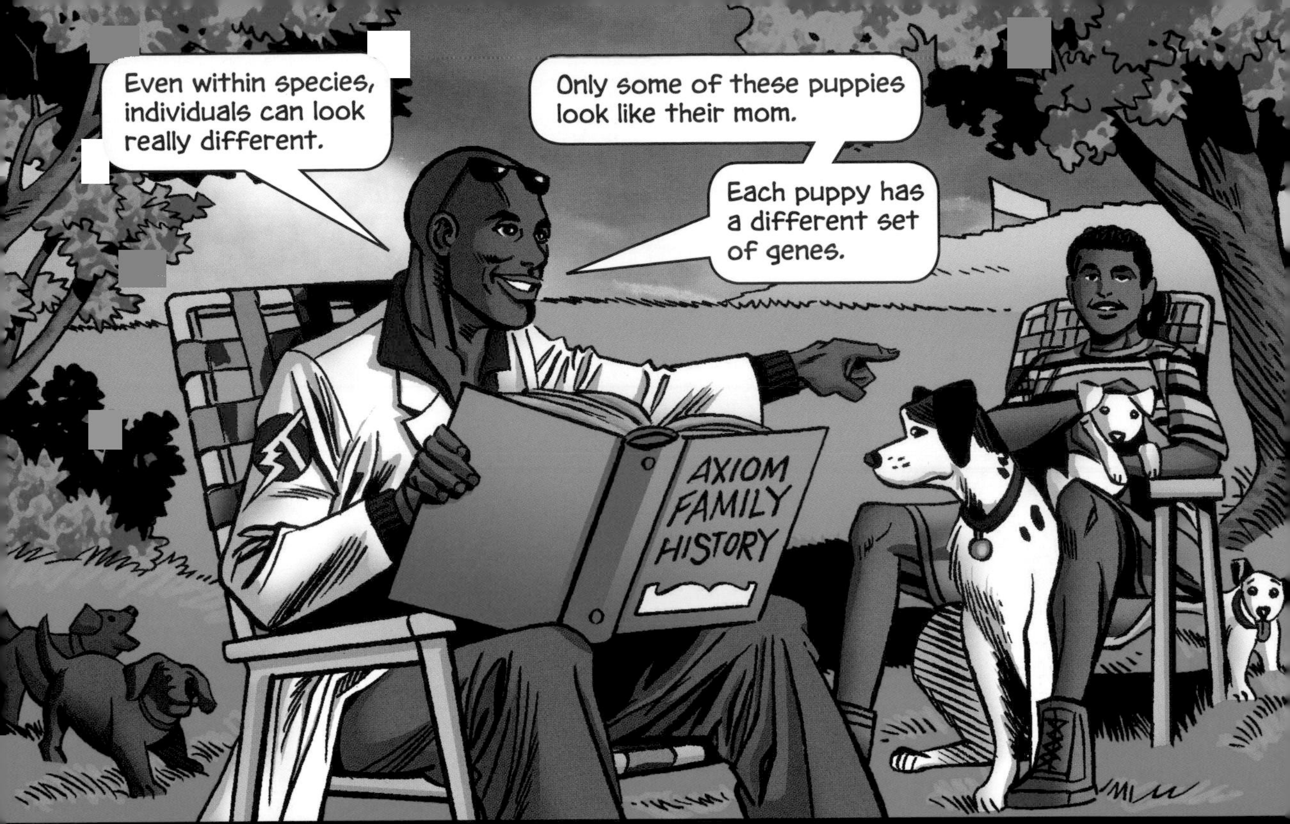
Even within species, individuals can look really different.
Only some of these puppies look like their mom.
Each puppy has a different set of genes.
AXIOM FAMILY HISTORY

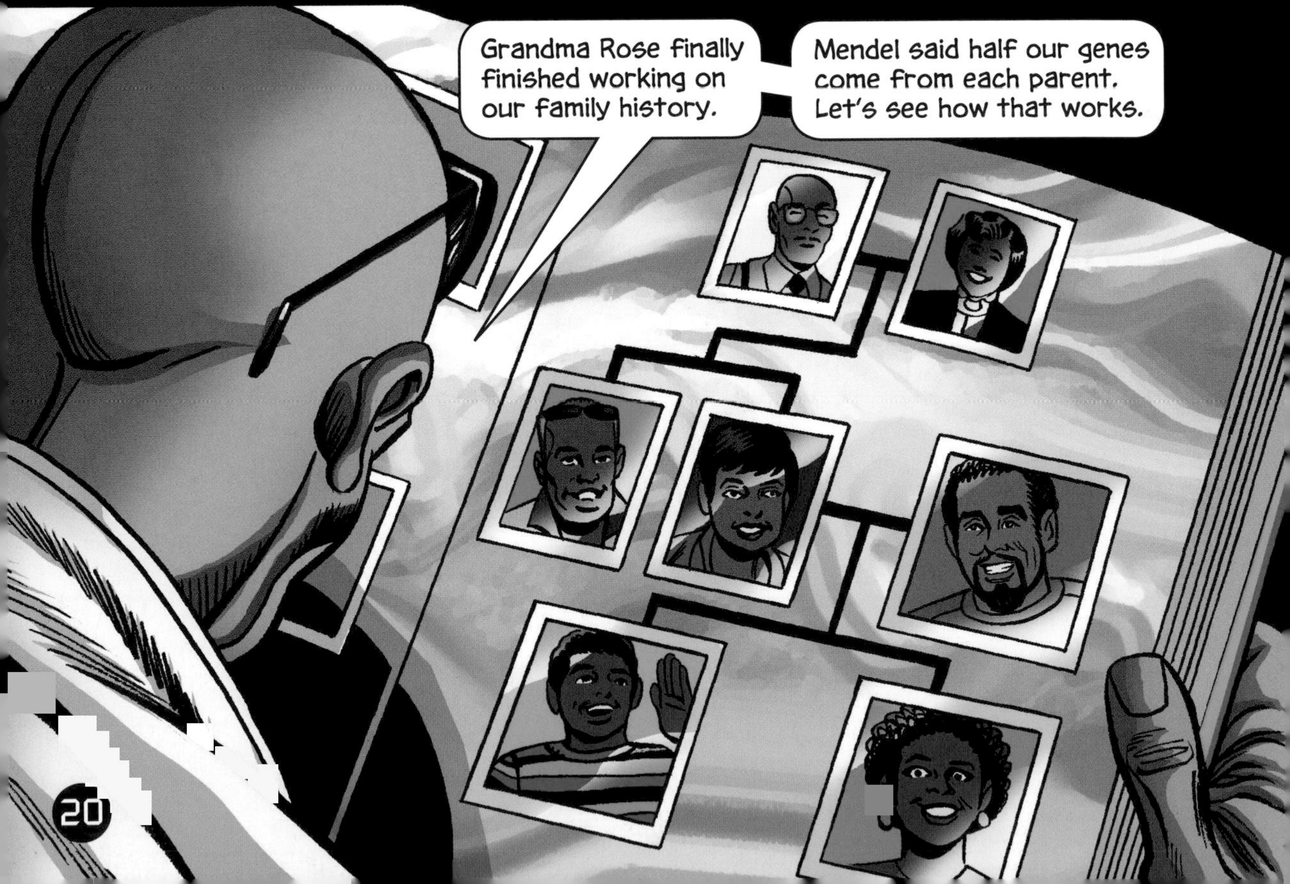
Grandma Rose finally finished working on our family history.
Mendel said half our genes come from each parent. Let's see how that works.

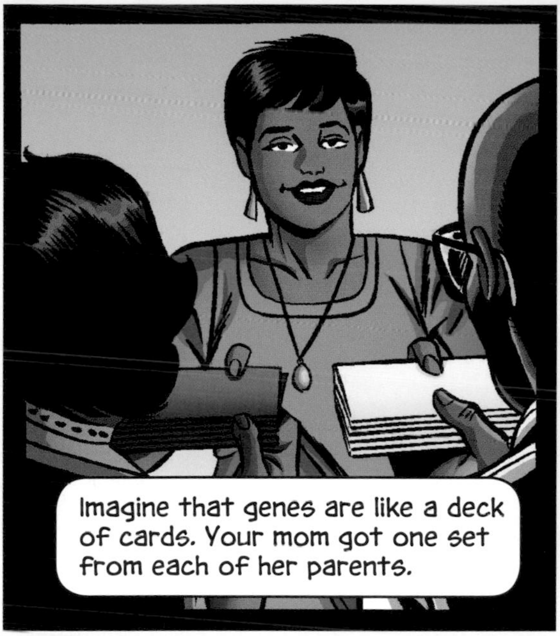
Imagine that genes are like a deck of cards. Your mom got one set from each of her parents.

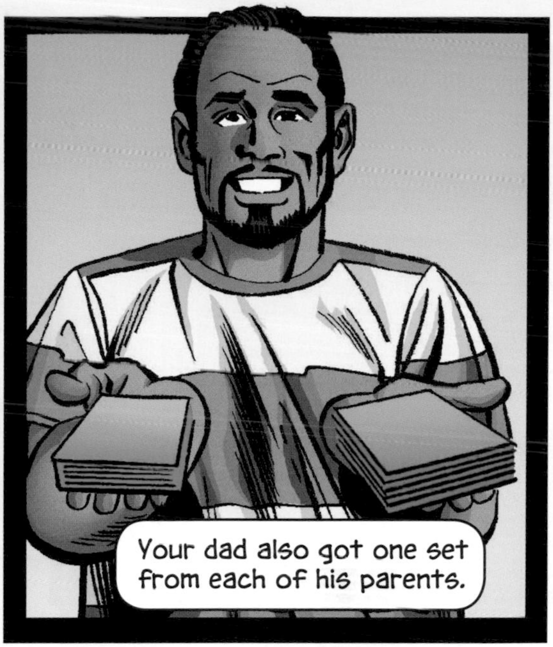
Your dad also got one set from each of his parents.

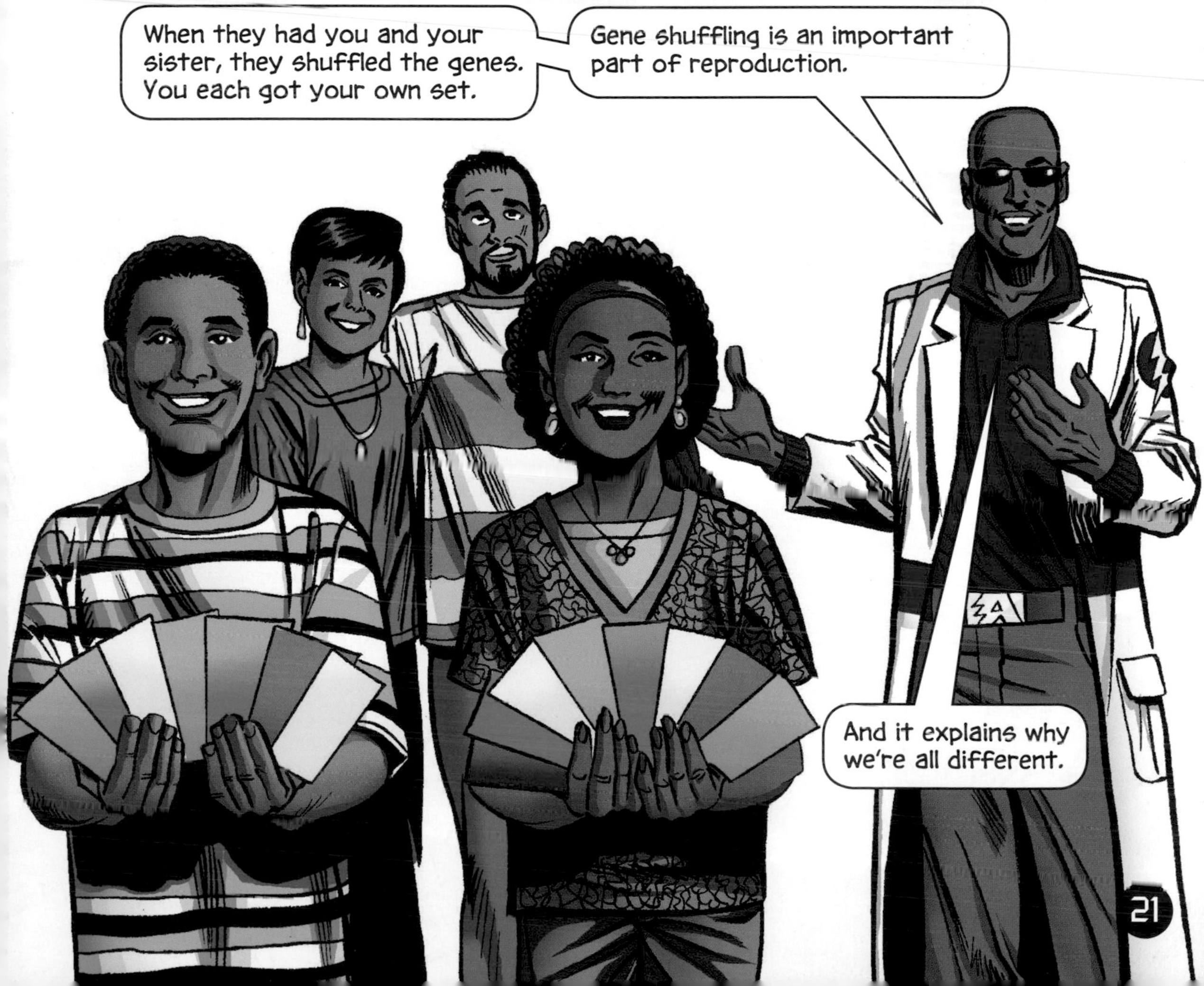
When they had you and your sister, they shuffled the genes. You each got your own set.
Gene shuffling is an important part of reproduction.
And it explains why we're all different.

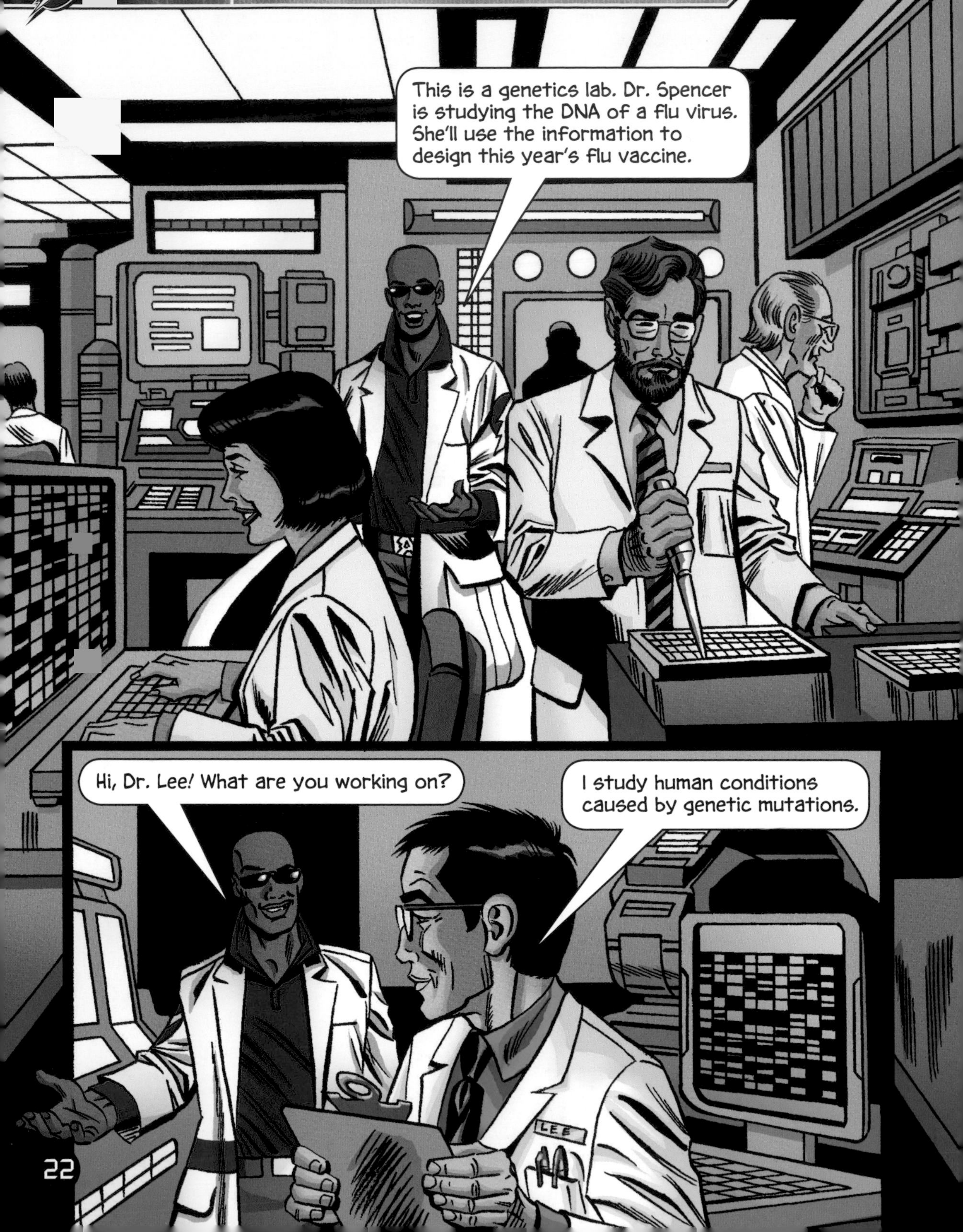
This is a genetics lab. Dr. Spencer is studying the DNA of a flu virus. She'll use the information to design this year's flu vaccine.
Hi, Dr. Lee! What are you working on?
I study human conditions caused by genetic mutations.
LEE

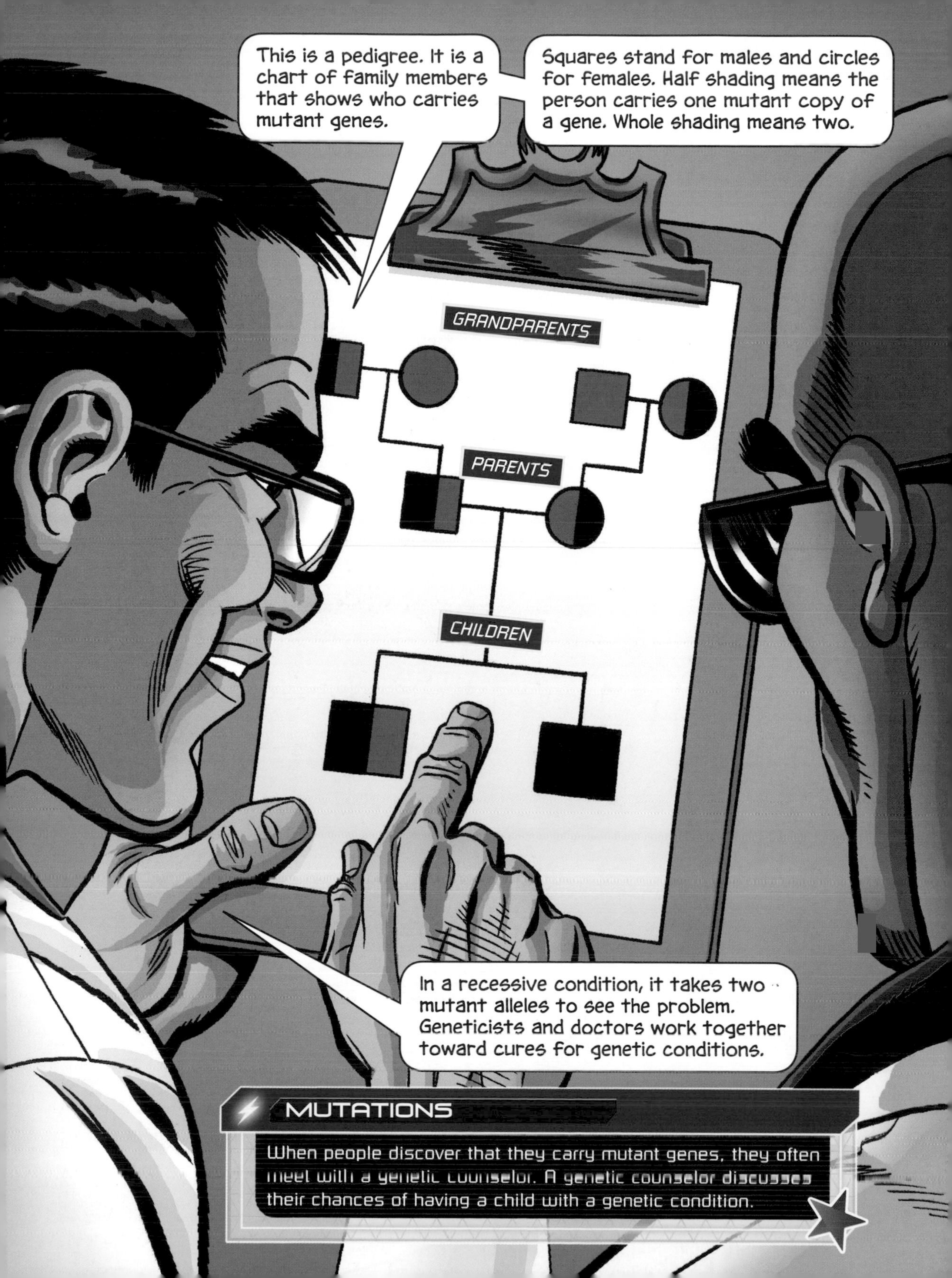

MUTATIONS

When people discover that they carry mutant genes, they often meet with a genetic counselor. A genetic counselor discusses their chances of having a child with a genetic condition.

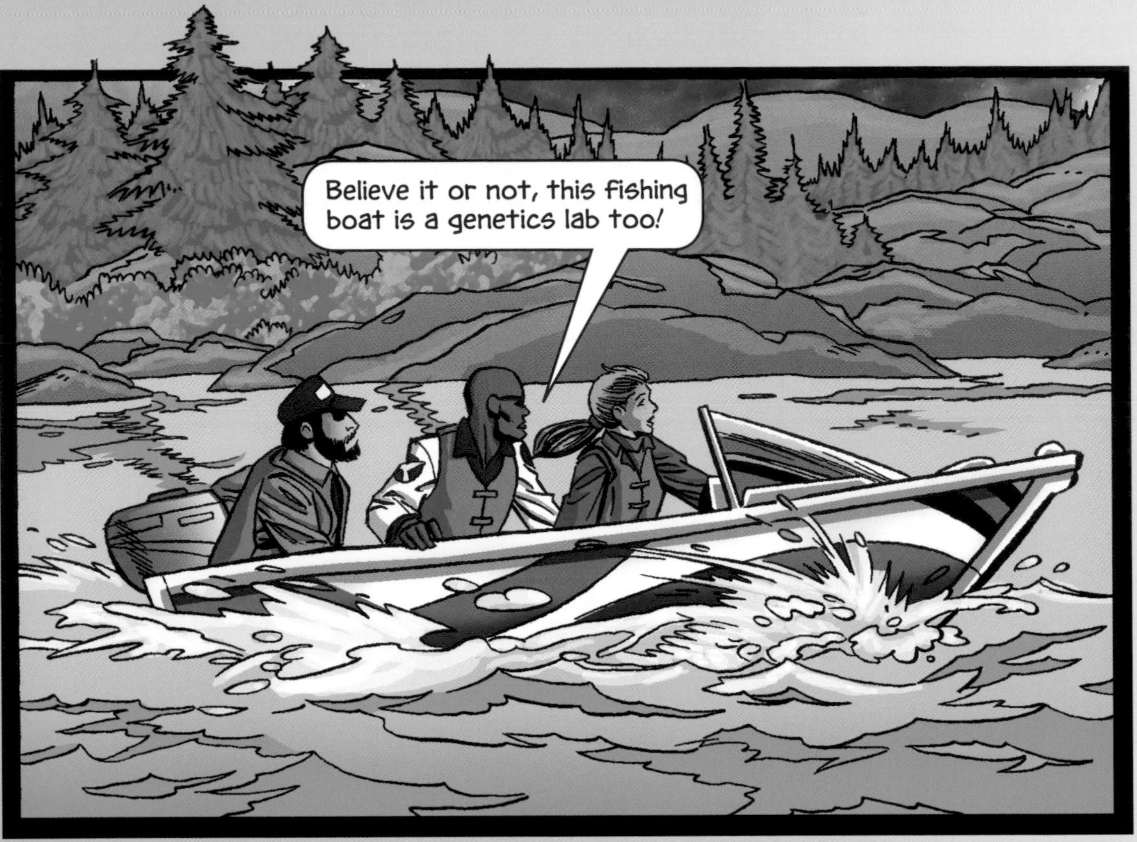
Believe it or not, this fishing boat is a genetics lab too!

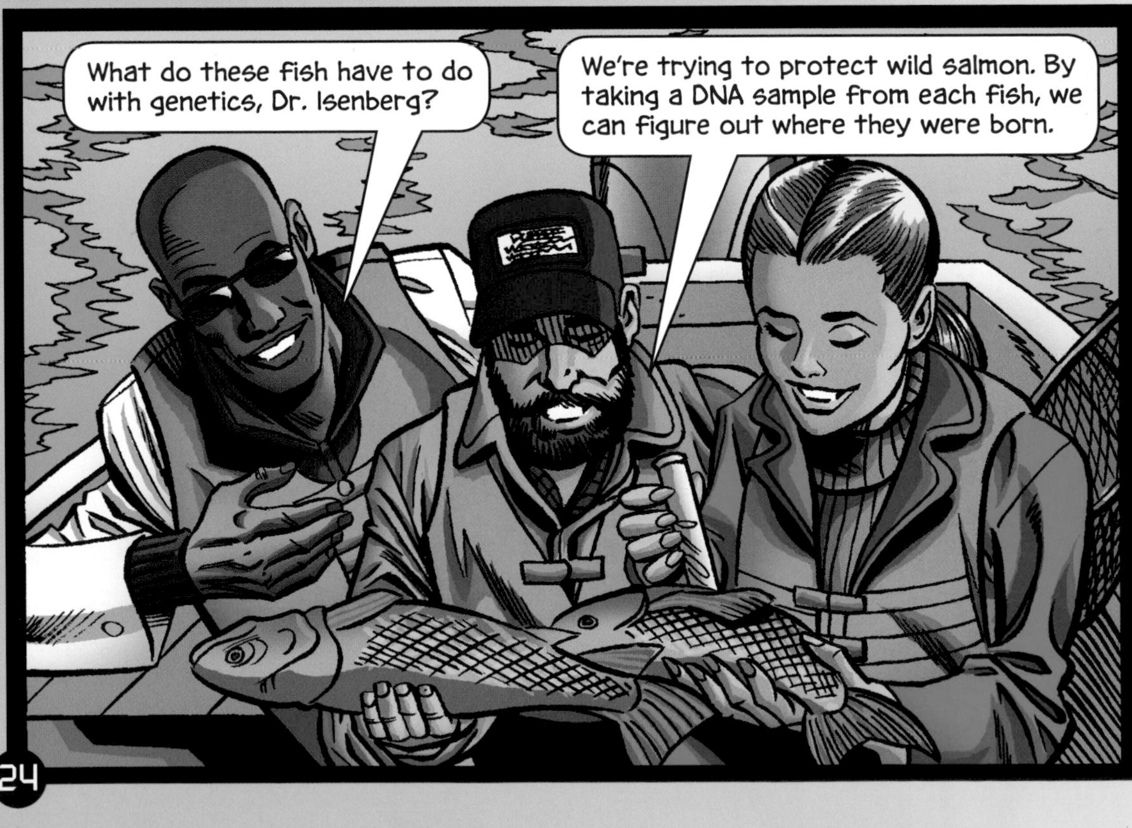
What do these fish have to do with genetics, Dr. Isenberg?
We're trying to protect wild salmon. By taking a DNA sample from each fish, we can figure out where they were born.

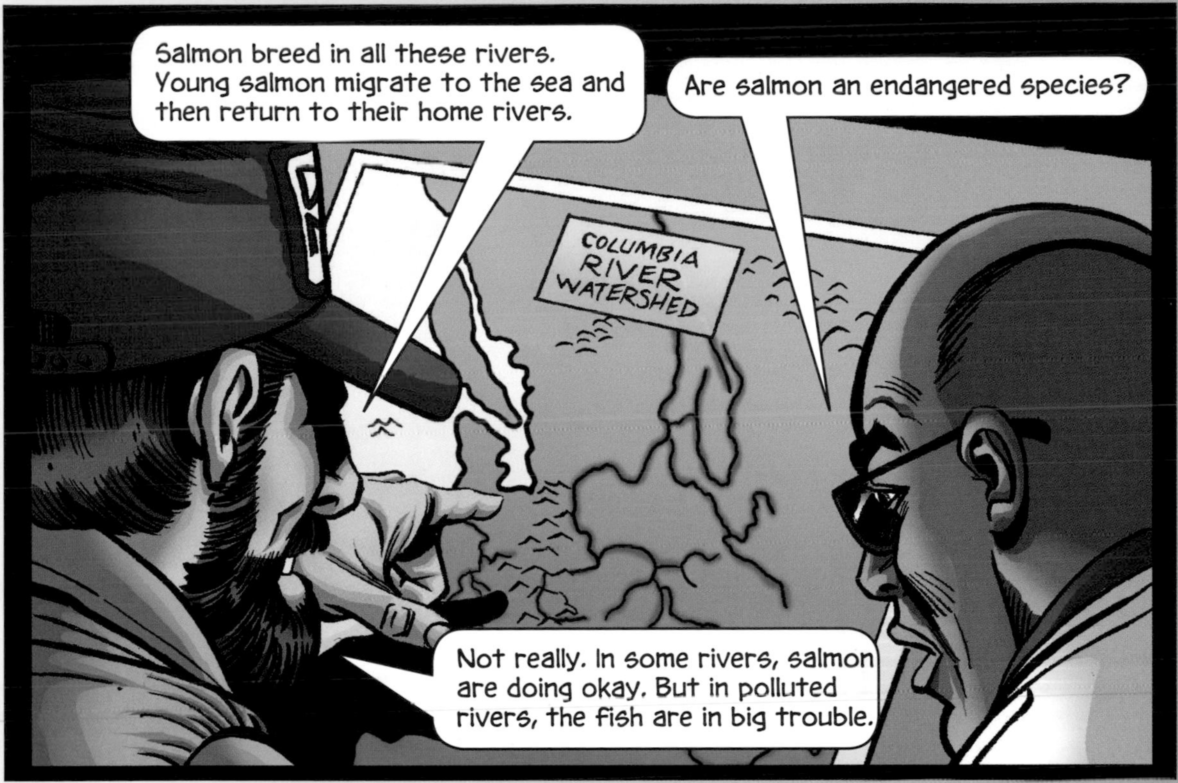
Salmon breed in all these rivers. Young salmon migrate to the sea and then return to their home rivers.
Are salmon an endangered species?
COLUMBIA RIVER WATERSHED
Not really. In some rivers, salmon are doing okay. But in polluted rivers, the fish are in big trouble.

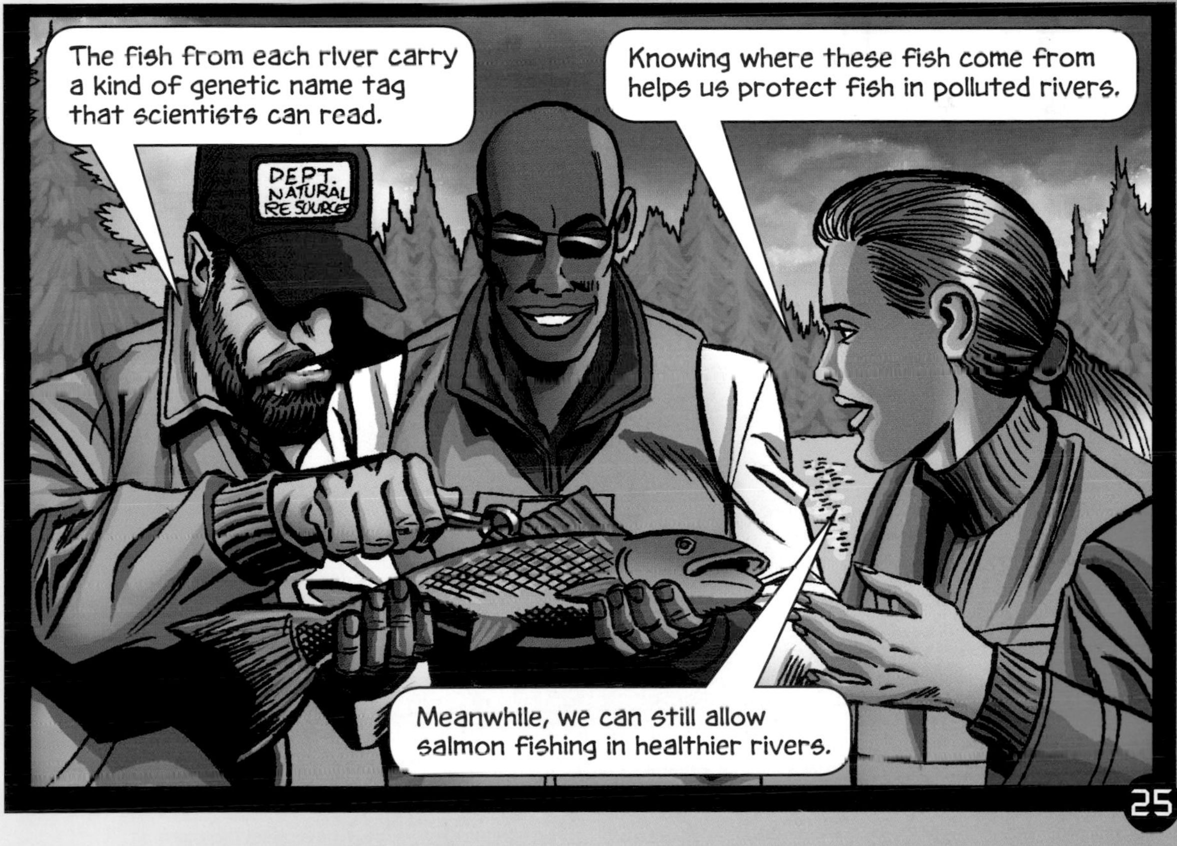
The fish from each river carry a kind of genetic name tag that scientists can read.
Knowing where these fish come from helps us protect fish in polluted rivers.
DEPT. NATURAL RESOURCES
Meanwhile, we can still allow salmon fishing in healthier rivers.

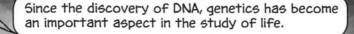

Since the discovery of DNA, genetics has become an important aspect in the study of life.

Genetic discoveries have influenced conservation, medicine, and farming.

This new knowledge raises ethical questions too.

Should we use DNA from living creatures to make exact copies or clones?

And what happens when we put new genes into these corn plants?

They may produce more food, but would it be safe to eat?

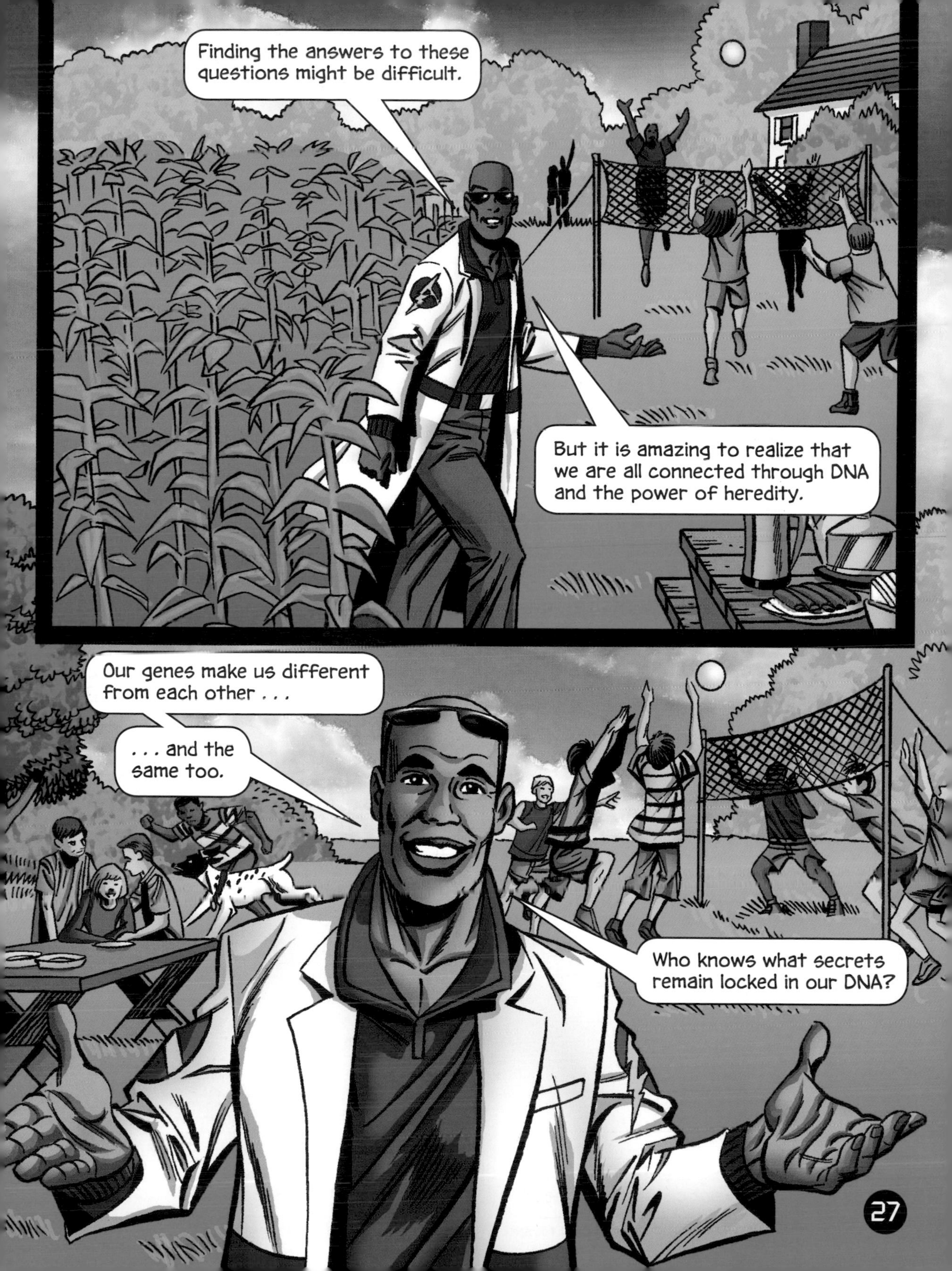
Finding the answers to these questions might be difficult.
But it is amazing to realize that we are all connected through DNA and the power of heredity.
Our genes make us different from each other . . .
. . . and the same too.
Who knows what secrets remain locked in our DNA?

Genotype is not the only thing that causes phenotype. Environment is important too. Even if a person has genes for being tall, without enough to eat, he'll be short.

The condition called Down syndrome occurs when a human child ends up with 47 chromosomes instead of 46.

To make Dolly, the famous sheep clone, scientists took a cell from an adult sheep and removed the DNA. They injected the DNA into an egg cell without any DNA. Then they put the egg inside of a female sheep where it grew into a new lamb. Dolly was an exact genetic copy of the first sheep.

Identical twins are a kind of clone. Very early in development, a fertilized egg splits in half. Each half grows into a baby. They are identical because each twin has exactly the same genes.

Many genes are necessary to tell cells when to divide and when to stop dividing. If a mutation occurs in any of those genes, cells will divide when they aren't supposed to. This results in the disease called cancer.

Genetic modification occurs when a scientist takes a gene from one organism and puts it into another. For example, a gene from bacteria was added to the corn genome. The gene makes a protein that kills caterpillars. The good thing is that farmers don't have to spray corn with insecticide. The bad thing is that the gene could spread to other plants and could even affect human health.

Some geneticists are trying to find cures for common genetic diseases using gene therapy. The idea is to replace damaged or mutated genes with normal ones.

There are many kinds of genetics. Some geneticists study the genomes of endangered species. Others try to understand how each individual gene gives directions to the body. They may also study phenotypes like height that are caused by many genes working together. Still others use genes to understand how groups of plants and animals have changed over time.

GUMMY DNA CHAIN

Four types of bases connect to make DNA: Adenine (A), Cytosine (C), Guanine (G), and Thymine (T). See how they work together by building your very own delicious gummy model of DNA.

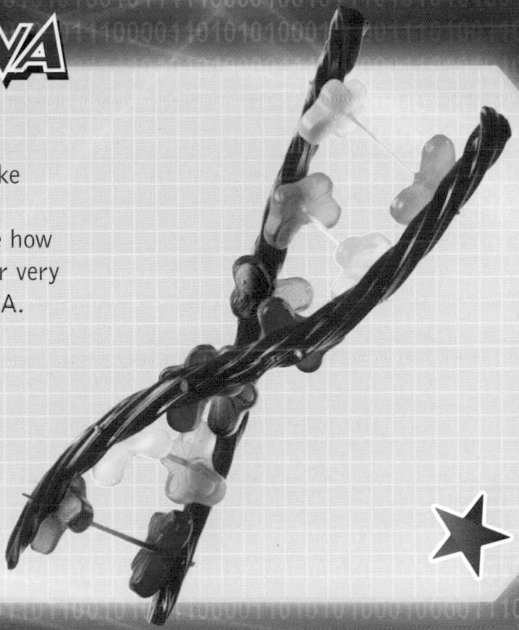

WHAT YOU NEED:

- paper
- marker
- gummy candies in four colors
- toothpicks
- licorice twists

WHAT YOU DO:

1. Using paper and a marker, create a chart that has four sections. Label them A, T, C, and G.

2. Choose four colors of gummy candies and assign each a letter from the DNA bases on your chart and sort them. The color you've chosen to be A will always pair with T, and the color you've chosen to be G will always pair with C.

3. Make a vertical row of about six gummy candies. You can add more if you want to make a longer DNA chain.

4. Create a second row of gummy candies with the same number, making sure each matches with the DNA base of the candy in the first row (A to T, G to C).

5. Use toothpicks to connect the gummies horizontally. Leave space on the ends of the toothpicks to connect to the licorice twists.

6. Connect one side of each pair of gummy candies to a licorice twist, leaving at least an inch (2.54 centimeters) of space between them. Connect the other licorice twist to the other side of the gummy pairs.

7. When everything is in place, twist the candy strings so they make a spiral. Your gummy DNA chain is complete. When you are done displaying it, take it apart and eat it!

DISCUSSION QUESTIONS

1. What is a trait? Discuss some physical traits you think a friend received from his or her parents.

2. What is a genome? What have scientists learned about different kinds of organisms by studying their genomes?

3. While microscopic, DNA has a unique appearance and composition. What does DNA look like? What is DNA made of?

4. What is the relationship between a gene and a protein? Between DNA and a chromosome? Discuss why these relationships are important.

WRITING PROMPTS

1. Compare and contrast an organism's genotype and phenotype. Write down some differences and similarities between them.

2. How can a child have her father's curly, brown hair and her mother's blue eyes? What makes this combination of traits possible?

3. Compare and contrast dominant and recessive genes. Then write a paragraph describing their differences and similarities.

4. Draw a picture of a pet you or a friend owns, such as a dog, cat, guinea pig, or fish. Then label and briefly describe each of that pet's physical traits.

TAKE A QUIZ!

GLOSSARY

allele (UH-lee-uhl)—one of two genes in a pair contributed by the parent

base (BAYS)—a building block of DNA; the four bases are adenine, guanine, thymine, and cytosine.

chromosome (KROH-muh-sohm)—a structure inside a cell containing genetic codes that control growth, development, and function of all cells

DNA (dee-en-AY)—the molecule that carries all of the instructions to make a living thing and keeps it working; short for deoxyribonucleic acid.

dominant (DOM-uh-nuhnt)—the gene most likely to produce a trait in offspring

gene (JEEN)—a part of every cell that carries physical and behavioral information passed from parents to their children

genetic mutation (juh-NET-ik myoo-TAY-shun)—a change in an animal's genetic makeup that causes it to develop in a different way

genotype (JEE-noh-tipe)—the genes that produce a phenotype

heredity (huh-RED-uh-tee)—the process by which parents pass traits to their children

nucleus (NOO-klee-uhss)—the part of each cell that contains the genetic material

phenotype (FEE-noh-tipe)—traits you can see, count, or measure

protein (PROH-teen)—a substance found in all living animal and plant cells; protein is necessary for growth and life.

recessive (ruh-SESS-iv)—the gene most likely to stay hidden in offspring

READ MORE

Anders, Mason. *DNA, Genes, and Chromosomes. Genetics.* North Mankato, MN: Capstone Press, 2017.

Easton, Marylin. *Dinosaur DNA: A Nonfiction Companion to the Films (Jurassic World): A Nonfiction Companion to the Films.* Jurassic World. New York, NY: Scholastic, Inc., 2018.

Taylor-Butler, Christine. *Genetics.* True Book. New York, NY: Children's Press, an imprint of Scholastic Inc., 2017.

INTERNET SITES

Easy Science for Kids: DNA: Your Body's Blueprints
https://easyscienceforkids.com/dna-your-bodys-blueprints/

KidsHealth: What is a Gene?
https://kidshealth.org/en/kids/what-is-gene.html

Your Genome: What is DNA?
https://www.yourgenome.org/facts/what-is-dna

Check out projects, games, and lots more at **www.capstonekids.com**

INDEX